Basic Classroom Skills
through Games

Related titles by the authors of
Basic Classroom Skills through Games

- *Basic Media Skills through Games*

- *Media Skills for Middle Grades*

Basic Classroom Skills through Games

Irene Wood Bell
Media Specialist
Denver Public Schools

Jeanne E. Wieckert
Media Specialist
Denver Public Schools

Illustrated by
Jay Conley

Libraries Unlimited, Inc.
Littleton, Colorado
1980

LIBRARIES UNLIMITED, INC.
P.O. Box 263
Littleton, Colorado 80160

Library of Congress Cataloging in Publication Data

Bell, Irene Wood, 1944-
    Basic classroom skills through games.

    Includes index.
    1. Educational games. I. Wieckert, Jeanne E.,
1939-   joint author. II. Conley, Jay. III. Title.
LB1029.G3B448   371.3   80-351
ISBN 0-87287-207-6

This book is bound with James River (Scott) Graphitek®—C Type II non-
woven material. Graphitek—C meets and exceeds National Association of
State Textbook Administrators' Type II nonwoven material specifications
Class A through E.

This book is dedicated to
our husbands: understanding,
encouraging and patient.

FOREWORD

Basic Classroom Skills through Games presents over 100 games that can be used in numerous combinations to teach a variety of skills in the classroom and in the media center. These games have grown from the authors' application of the teaching methods exemplified in *Basic Media Skills through Games* (Libraries Unlimited, 1979) to skills students acquire in the classroom. They are designed to introduce students to the language arts, reading, social studies, and specialist areas, and some, like those in the companion volume, are designed to enable elementary school students to use the IMC (Instructional Media Center) more effectively. Target skills include alphabetizing; understanding the logic and use of dictionaries and encyclopedias; identifying other reference books and their uses; understanding the functions and applications of maps, globes, and atlases; and developing a familiarity with and appreciation of literature.

Within each of the five sections of the book, games are presented in a sequence beginning with introductory games for the primary grades and moving through games for the sixth grade which approach more advanced concepts and reinforce the basic skills. As with those in *Basic Media Skills through Games*, each game in this volume has been tested and refined by the authors in their respective media centers before it ever found its way onto paper, and each has been found to contribute to students' using the IMC to their best advantage.

The key to using *Basic Classroom Skills through Games* effectively is to employ the variety of types of games and their adaptability to a wide range of situations. There are card games, dice games, board games, puzzles, hands-on games, location games, and identification games. All make use of inexpensive materials that are readily available in most schools, and once a game is set up, it can be used repeatedly. Variations of games are suggested in many cases, which expands their applicability. Some games involve team efforts, while others call for individual responses. Many can be used as either a team or an individual exercise, depending upon the needs of any given group.

Teachers and media specialists will find that a particular game may have more immediate application to some areas of the curriculum than to others. The explanation of the purpose of each game, included both in the table of contents and in the presentation of the game, is designed to aid the teacher in choosing the combination of games that will be most efficient in the presentation of a particular skill. The authors have included, for instance, quite a few games designed to develop skills related to the alphabet. "On Safari," "Pic

Mix," and "Can You Find???," all of which promote familiarity with the letters themselves and the sounds they designate, are most clearly applicable to the language arts. "Authors' Initials," on the other hand, is a letter game that allows students to develop and demonstrate an initial familiarity with literature. "Alphabet Race," "Author Scramble," and "Cracker Jack" will develop the alphabetizing skills that will grant students more immediate access to information in reference works. The combination and adaptation of these games should allow the teacher to approach skills in many curriculum areas.

The elements of competition and cooperation have been found to be very effective in transmitting and reinforcing skills, and for this reason, games are structured so that winners (teams or individuals) can emerge, which always adds an air of interest for students. (Teachers or specialists can decide whether or not actual prizes will be awarded, and some may wish to use points to help determine grades.) Some games require checking on results by the teacher or specialist, while others require the students to check themselves or each other (with the teacher or specialist available as arbiter). In all, the potential uses of the games to teach and reinforce skills depend solely upon the needs and imagination of the teacher or specialist.

Although the lists of materials and instructions for each game are essentially complete and self-contained, a few games will refer to materials or procedures presented before. Such references are clearly noted in the listing of materials for any games of this nature. Beyond this and the general principles of variety and adaptability, a few guidelines must be set. Noting these points prior to setting up the games for actual play will possibly prevent confusion, inconvenience, or destruction of materials. First, the game to be used should be read thoroughly by the teacher or specialist far enough in advance that there will be time to make the materials—some will require a few hours to prepare. Also, keeping the book handy during play will help if consultation of the rules in some of the more complex games is required. Paper materials (whether of posterboard, oak-tag board, index cards, etc.) can and should be laminated in advance of play to ensure their survival if multiple use is desired (clear contact paper or "Seal Laminating Film" will suffice). Gameboards can be copied directly from the book. The easiest method is to use an opaque projector to project the board on a piece of posterboard taped to a wall; the gameboard can then simply be traced over the projected image. The choice of eraseable (Vis-a-Vis®) pens was made to facilitate repeated use of materials; non-eraseable (Sharpie®) pens are suggested when materials are to be of a permanent nature. (Any pens of similar qualities can be used, of course.)

The games lend themselves to any number of adaptations and variations. In many cases, the level of difficulty can be altered by substituting different questions or lists. Card games and puzzles dealing with authors and book titles can be adapted to a particular group's interests by substituting their selections of favorite books or an endless variety of other lists. Each teacher or specialist will suggest adaptations to his or her own students, materials, and operations, and the authors encourage teachers or specialists to make the games relevent to students' immediate situations.

Once the materials are assembled, establishing basic procedures within the classroom can help to eliminate potential problems. Most important, the teacher or specialist should explain the game to students thoroughly at the outset and make sure that all students understand the rules before proceeding. When teams are called for, instructions often require that a team leader be chosen; the method for doing so is often left to the discretion of the teacher or specialist, as some will prefer to appoint leaders while others may prefer that students select from among themselves (by any number of processes). Similarly, teachers or specialists may wish to alter the suggested methods of determining order of play; the authors frequently suggest alphabetical order by last name, but any method that demonstrates impartiality (e.g., drawing lots) would be acceptable. As for direction of play around a circle, going to the left or right is optional, naturally, so long as it is done consistently and does not confuse students or interfere with play. Finally, instructions include directions that students replace materials in the containers provided, but the teacher or specialist will want to review any previously used game's materials prior to replay in order to be sure that all parts are present and in good enough repair to use.

Keeping all these principles in mind should allow for the fewest unwelcome surprises. Careful and thoughtful use of *Basic Classroom Skills through Games* will allow the teacher or specialist to structure a program of activities that presents students with the opportunity to learn. The only surprise may be how quickly and enthusiastically they do so.

I.W.B.
J.E.W.

TABLE OF CONTENTS

PART I — 26 LITTLE LETTERS:
The Alphabet

Since the beginning of time, and especially with the explosion of knowledge in the middle of the 20th century, man has been continually sorting and categorizing — finding an order. Probably one of the first categories or orders a child is exposed to in school is the alphabet. As early as three or four years of age, children are learning letters and the particular order they come in. But this is not enough. As the child matures he/she must learn the sound for each letter, must learn to write the symbol for each letter, and must learn to put the letters together to form words. Beyond this he/she must learn the beginning, middle, and end of the alphabet. He/she must be able to put words in order using first letter, second letter, third letter, and so on. Also, the child must be able to recognize letters coming before and after another letter.

There is a complex set of sequential skills that need to be acquired by children as they learn to alphabetize. The games and activities presented in this chapter, if followed in the order in which they are presented, will help a child enjoy learning the alphabet and its related areas.

BIBLIOGRAPHY

Alexander, Anne. *ABC of Cars and Trucks*. Garden City, NY, Doubleday, 1956.

Anglund, Joan Walsch. *A Mother Goose ABC in a Pumpkin Shell*. New York, Harcourt Brace and World, 1960.

Asimov, Isaac. *ABC's of Space*. New York, Walker, 1969.

Bowman, Clare. *Busy Bodies: The Busy ABC's*. Eau Claire, WI, E. M. Hall, 1964.

Brown, Marcia. *All Butterflies*. New York, Charles Scribner's Sons, 1974.

Charlip, Remy. *Handtalk: An ABC of Finger Spelling & Sign Language*. New York, Parent's Magazine Press, 1974.

Charles, Donald. *Letters from Calico Cat*. Chicago, Children's Press, 1974.

Children's TV Workshop, ed. *Sesame Street Book of Letters*. Boston, Little Brown, 1970.

Cleary, Beverly. *The Hullabalo ABC*. Berkeley, CA, Parnassus Press, 1960.

Crews, Donald. *We Read A to Z*. New York, Harper & Row, 1967.

Fife, Dale. *Adam's ABC*. New York, Coward, McCann & Geoghegan, 1971.

Gag, Wanda. *The ABC Bunny*. New York, Coward, McCann & Geoghegan, 1933.

Geisel, Theodor Seuss. *Dr. Seuss's ABC*. New York, Random House, 1963.

Guthrie, Vee. *Animals from A to Z*. New York, Van Nostrand Reinhold, 1969.

Lord, Beman. *Our Baby's ABC*. New York, Henry Z. Walck, 1964.

Miller, Albert G. *Backward Beasts from A to Z*. Glendale, CA, Bowmar, 1974.

Miller, Albert G. *Talking Letters*. Glendale, CA, Bowmar, 1974.

Miller, Edna. *Mousekin's ABC*. Englewood Cliffs, NJ, Prentice-Hall, 1972.

Peppé, Rodney. *The Alphabet Book*. New York, Four Winds Press, 1968.

Rockwell, Anne. *Albert B. Cub & Zebra; An Alphabet Storybook*. New York, Thomas Y. Crowell, 1977.

Rojankovsky, Feodor. *Animals in the Zoo*. New York, Alfred A. Knopf, 1962.

Sendak, Maurice. *Alligators All Around*. New York, Harper & Row, 1962.

Taylor, Margaret C. *Wht's Yr Nm?* New York, Harcourt Brace and World, 1970.

◄►◄►◄►◄►◄►◄►◄►◄►◄►◄►◄►◄►◄►◄►◄►◄►◄►◄►
LOWER-CASE LETTERS
◄►◄►◄►◄►◄►◄►◄►◄►◄►◄►◄►◄►◄►◄►◄►◄►◄►◄►

PURPOSE: To familiarize students with lower-case letters and their positions in the alphabet.

GRADE LEVEL: Primary—1st grade

TIME: 25 minutes

NUMBER: Best played with a maximum of 16 students

METHOD OF CHECKING: Teacher

MATERIALS:
1) Three or more pieces of colored posterboard cut into 9x24-inch strips.
   a) On each strip make two black horizontal lines, 3-inches apart.
   b) Between the lines on these cards print the lower-case letters using a black felt-tipped pen, making sure the letters touch the lines.

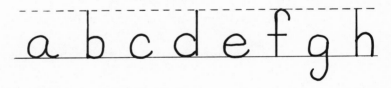

2) Master list of questions and answers dry-mounted to a piece of colored posterboard:

   Which letter is curved like a wriggling snake and makes a sound like a hissing snake? (s)

   If it rained on these letters, which ones would hold water? (k, u, v, w, x, y)

   Which letters have tails hanging down below the line? (g, j, p, q, y, z)

   Which letters have only straight lines in them? (k, l, v, w, x, y)

(Materials list continues on page 24)

Which letters have only curved lines in them? (c, o, s)

Which letters have both straight and curved lines in them? (a, b, d, e, f, g, h, j, m, n, p, q, r, t, u)

Which letters have points in them? (k, v, w, x, y, z)

Does a "g" look like a "q"? What differences do you see between them?

Does a lower-case "q" look like a lower-case "o"? What is the difference?

The letters "b" and "d" sound somewhat alike. Do they look alike? What is the difference?

"m" and "n" also sound somewhat alike. They almost look alike. The letter "m" has something that "n" does not have. What is it?

What two letters require a dot over them? (i, j)

The letters "p" and "q" look alike. What is the difference?

What letter looks like an upside down mountain peak? (v)

What is the difference between "a" and "o"?

How can you tell an "n" from a "u"?

How are "m" and "w" alike?

How can you tell a "v" from a "w"?

What seven letters are taller than all the others? (b, d, f, h, k, l, t)

What four letters look the same when they are upside down? (l, o, x, z)

What two sets of letters in alphabetical order spell a two-letter word? (hi, no)

If you turn "b" upside down, what letter do you have? (q)

What letter looks like a circle that's not quite finished? (c)

How are "g" and "j" the same?

How are "u" and "v" different?

How are "h" and "n" alike?

What letter looks like a capital N that is sleeping? (z)

What letter would look like a straight line if it fell over on its side? (l)

What is the difference between "r" and "n"?

3)   Large manila envelope (12x15-inches) for the materials.

PROCEDURE:

1) Display the alphabet, in lower-case letters, at the students' eye level.

2) Arrange the students in a circle on the floor.

3) Go around the circle of students in a clockwise direction asking the questions listed on the master list.

4) As the letters are discussed, have the students name them and point to them.

5) For each question answered and letters pointed to correctly, the student scores a point.

■ ■ ■

ALPHA CONCENTRATION

PURPOSE: To familiarize students with capital and lower-case letters.

GRADE LEVEL: Primary—1st and 2nd grades

TIME: 25 minutes each for Forms A, B, and C

NUMBER: Best played with a maximum of 16 students

METHOD OF CHECKING: Teacher

MATERIALS:

1) FORM A—3 sets of 52 3x4-inch colored posterboard cards bearing two complete sets of capital letters, one letter per card.

2) FORM B—3 sets of 52 3x4-inch colored posterboard cards bearing two complete sets of lower-case letters, one letter per card.

3) FORM C—3 sets of 52 3x4-inch colored posterboard cards bearing one complete set of capital letters and one complete set of lower-case letters. (A total of 156 cards are needed for each form.)

FORM A

FORM B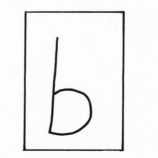

FORM C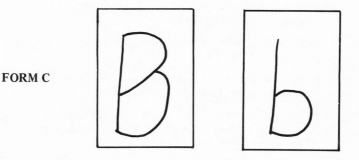

4) Large manila envelope (12x15-inches) for the materials.

PROCEDURE:

FORM A

1) Four to six players gather around a table or in a circle on the floor in alphabetical order by the first initials of their last names. If there is more than one student per initial, alphabetize by the second letter.

2) The player with the initial closest to the beginning of the alphabet is the dealer.

3) Dealer shuffles cards and places the cards face down on the table or floor. The cards may be laid out in any pattern, but no two cards should touch each other.

4) Note: each player must try to remember the position of each card on the table or floor.

5) The dealer starts the game by turning face up any two cards, one at a time. All the players look at the two cards as they are turned up. The two cards are not picked up, just turned face up.

6) If the two cards are a pair, the dealer picks them up, keeps them, and turns up two more cards. The dealer's turn continues as long as the two cards turned up are a pair. A pair consists of two matching capital letters. For example, A and A would make a pair.

7) If the two cards are not a pair, they are turned face down and left in their original places. This ends the dealer's turn. (Note: cards are picked up only when they are a pair.)

8) After the dealer's turn is over, the player to the left of the dealer continues the game. Play continues around the table to the left.

9) Each player tries to remember which cards are turned up and their exact locations. Remembering where the cards are can help a player win the game. For example, suppose that B was turned up, but was not paired with another card. It was turned face down. If a player turns up a B and remembers the location of the first B, a pair is matched.

(Procedures continue on page 28)

10) Every time a pair is turned up, the player picks them up, keeps them, and continues to try to match cards.

11) A player's turn ends when two cards that are not a pair are turned up.

12) At the end of the game, each player scores one point for each matched pair in front of him/her.

13) The winner is the player who has accumulated the greatest number of pairs after all the cards have been picked up from the table or floor.

FORM B

The same as Form A except the pairs to be matched will be lower-case letters.

FORM C

The same as Form A except the players will match capital letters to their lower-case forms.

■ ■ ■

BEFORE AND AFTER BASEBALL

PURPOSE: To promote facility in using alphabet letters by learning to identify the letters before and after a particular letter in the alphabet.

GRADE LEVEL: Primary—1st and 2nd grades

TIME: 25 minutes

NUMBER: Best played with a maximum of 16 students

METHOD OF CHECKING: Teacher

MATERIALS:

1) 1 set of bases and a homerun plate—total of four cloth bags or posterboard cards. A chalkboard with a baseball diamond may also be used.

2) 1 set of 3x3-inch colored posterboard alphabet cards with the letters B through Y printed on them—24 cards.

3) Large manila envelope (16x20-inches) for the materials.

PROCEDURE:

1) Set up a small baseball diamond to have players actually move to bases or draw a diamond on the chalkboard to indicate movement around the bases.

2) Divide the students into two evenly matched teams.

3) The team whose captain's last name begins with the letter closest to the beginning of the alphabet will be at bat first. The team lines up behind the captain.

4) Place a set of alphabet letters face down in front of the team. The first player on team one must choose a letter and give the letter that comes before it and after it. (Example: C—B and D)

5) If correct, the player moves to first base. If incorrect, the player goes to the end of the line.

6) Each correct answer moves a player to first base, causing others to advance to second, third or home plate, thus scoring a run.

7) When a player has rounded all bases, he/she goes to the end of the line until his/her turn "at bat" comes up again.

8) Team one continues until it gets three outs (three wrong answers): then team two has a turn at bat.

9) Teams alternate play in this manner.

10) The team that scores the most runs is the winner.

■ ■ ■

PURPOSE: To promote skill in letter identification and letter information.

GRADE LEVEL: Primary—1st and 2nd grades

TIME: 25 minutes

NUMBER: Best played with a maximum of 16 students

METHOD OF CHECKING: Teacher

MATERIALS:
1) Chalk and chalkboard for keeping score.
2) Alphabet on display.

PROCEDURE:
1) Divide the students into two evenly matched teams.

2) The teacher chooses a number from 1 to 10, in order to determine team order of play.

3) The first student on each team is to guess a number between 1 and 10. The number that matches (or is closest to) the number that the teacher has written down designates which team goes first.

4) A student from team one comes to the front and stands with his/her back to team two.

5) The player raises a hand above his/her head and "writes" a letter in the air.

6) The first student on team two must correctly identify the letter to get a point for the team.

7) If the letter is correctly identified, it is team two's turn to "write" a letter in the air for team one.

8) If the student does not identify the letter, a point is given to team one, and the second student on team one takes a turn.

9) The game continues in this fashion until everyone receives a turn or until the end of the period.

10) The team with the most points wins.

LETTER HOP SCOTCH

PURPOSE: To give practice in letter identification.

GRADE LEVEL: Primary — 1st and 2nd grades

TIME: Form A — 25 minutes; Form B — 25 minutes

NUMBER: Best played with a maximum of 16 students

METHOD OF CHECKING: Teacher

MATERIALS:
1) 4 hopscotch figures with letters printed in boxes. A heavy clear plastic, such as used to cover "good" tablecloths, works best. Masking tape on the carpet or floor with felt letters is an alternative.

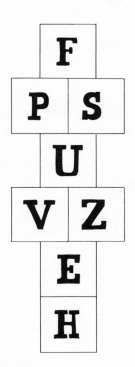

Note: alphabet may include upper case and lower case letters.

2) 4 9x12-inch oak-tag score boards in the forms of the hop scotch figures.

(Materials list continues on page 32)

3)   4 Vis-a-Vis® marking pens.

4)   Damp paper towels.

5)   Large manila envelope (16x20-inches) for the materials.

PROCEDURE:
FORM A

1)   The teacher chooses four captains and each captain chooses three students for his/her team.

2)   Each captain is assigned to a hop-scotch figure and is put in charge of scoring on the oak-tag score board.

3)   The first player hops on the bottom square and names the letter (hops like in hop scotch). If correct, the player hops until he/she is either out or reaches the end. If incorrect, the player is out, goes to the end of the line, and receives no score. Then the second player starts.

4)   When every team member has completed a turn, the teams rotate to different figures. This rotation is repeated after each round of turns. Each group rotates to a different figure to gain practice in all the letters.

5)   If a player reaches the end of the figure, he/she scores 10 points.

6)   The team with the most points, at the end of the game, is the winner.

FORM B

Played like Form A except that the player must give a word beginning with the letter hopped on.

■ ■ ■

ON SAFARI

PURPOSE: To give practice in identifying the beginning letter of a word.

GRADE LEVEL: Primary—1st and 2nd grades

TIME: 25 minutes

NUMBER: Best played with a maximum of 16 students

METHOD OF CHECKING: Teacher

MATERIALS:

1) Pictures of animals that begin with each letter of the alphabet, excluding "u" and "x."

2) Dry-mount pictures to pieces of colored posterboard.

3) Clothesline or wire.

4) Clothes pins.

5) Large manila envelope (16x20-inches) for the materials.

PROCEDURES:

1) Prior to the students arrival, hang the animal pictures on the wire around the room.

2) Divide the students into two evenly matched teams. A team captain is appointed by the teacher.

3) Each team lines up behind its respective team captain.

4) The teacher says, "I am thinking of an animal that starts with the letter B."

5) The team captains go "on safari" to find the picture of an animal that begins with the letter B.

6) The first captain to find the picture brings it to the teacher, tells what it is, and receives a point for the team.

7) Teams continue in relay fashion until all the letters have been used and all the pictures found or time runs out.

8) The team with the most points, at the end of the period, is the winner.

■ ■ ■

PURPOSE: To give practice in identifying beginning letters.

GRADE LEVEL: Primary—1st grade

TIME: 25 minutes

NUMBER: Best played with a maximum of 16 students

METHOD OF CHECKING: Teacher

MATERIALS:
1) 4 shoeboxes.
2) 4 objects for each letter of the alphabet—they need not be identical. For example,

acorn	button	crayon	die
eraser	fork	glass	jack
key	pencil	toothpick	zipper

3) Store the objects in the shoeboxes so that the complete alphabet is represented in each box.

PROCEDURE:
1) The teacher chooses four captains and each captain chooses three students for his/her team.
2) Each group of four sits in a circle on the floor.
3) A box containing 26 small objects is given to the captain.
4) Each captain places the objects on the floor in the center.
5) The teacher calls out a letter and all players attempt to find the object matching that letter.
6) The first student to hold the correct object overhead wins a point for the team.
7) The object is then placed back in the box, and play continues until all the objects have been picked.
8) The team with the most points when all the letters have been called wins.

■ ■ ■

◄►
PIC MIX
◄►

PURPOSE: To give practice in identifying beginning letters.

GRADE LEVEL: Primary — 1st and 2nd grades

TIME: 25 minutes

NUMBER: Best played with a maximum of 16 students

METHOD OF CHECKING: Teacher

MATERIALS:
1) 4 shoeboxes.

2) 4 sets of 3x4-inch colored posterboard alphabet cards. 26 letters to a set for a total of 104 cards.

3) 4 sets of 3x4-inch colored posterboard cards with pictures that match the alphabet; they may be pictures of animals, birds, flowers, and so on. 26 pictures per set for a total of 104 cards.

4) Store each set in a shoebox.

PROCEDURE:
1) Students count off in fours and divide into four groups around four tables.

2) One set of alphabet cards and one of picture cards are laid out face down on each table in any configuration.

3) Players take turns going clockwise around the tables.

4) Player A turns over two cards. If the name of the picture begins with the letter of the card drawn, the player keeps the pair and turns over two more. If they do not match, the cards are turned face down again.

5) Player B takes his/her turn and follows the same procedure. Then players C and D take their turns.

6) Players continue to take turns until all the cards are matched.

7) The player with the most correctly matched pairs, at the end of the game, is the winner.

■ ■ ■

◄► ◄► ◄► ◄► ◄► ◄► ◄► ◄► ◄► ◄► ◄► ◄► ◄► ◄► ◄► ◄► ◄► ◄► ◄► ◄►
I'M GOING TO . . .
◄► ◄► ◄► ◄► ◄► ◄► ◄► ◄► ◄► ◄► ◄► ◄► ◄► ◄► ◄► ◄► ◄► ◄► ◄► ◄►

PURPOSE: To give practice in matching words with the letters they begin with.

GRADE LEVEL: Primary—2nd and 3rd grades

TIME: Form A—25 minutes; Form B—25 minutes

NUMBER: Best played with a maximum of 16 students

METHOD OF CHECKING: Teacher

MATERIALS:
Depending on what categories will be used, have available: pictures, maps, books, and so on although they will only supplement the game.

PROCEDURE:
FORM A

1) One person is chosen to come to the front of the group and say: "I'm going to . . . " any town, city, state, country, and so on beginning with the letter A.

2) The player then calls on a student in the group and begins counting to 10 (out loud).

3) While the counting is going on, the student called on must name three words that start with A.

4) If the student names three words beginning with A before the count of ten, it is his/her turn and he/she must choose a place beginning with another letter.

5) If the student fails to name three words beginning with A, the original player receives a second turn and must choose a place beginning with another letter.

6) The game continues until all the letters of the alphabet are used or until time is called.

FORM B

The same procedure is followed as for Form A, but the student who is called on is limited to giving three words in a particular category. Names of animals, insects, flowers, book characters, items found in a supermarket, and so on. Allow students to look through available materials for ideas.

36

◄►
CAN YOU FIND???
◄►

PURPOSE: To acquaint students with letters of the alphabet, words beginning with those letters and pictures of objects beginning with those letters.

GRADE LEVEL: Primary—1st grade

TIME: Form A—25 minutes; Form B—25 minutes

NUMBER: Best played with a maximum of 16 students

METHOD OF CHECKING: Teacher

MATERIALS:

1) One die.

2) 50 5x5-inch colored posterboard cards with words.

3) 50 5x5-inch colored posterboard cards with pictures of objects named on the word cards.

4) Words for Form A:

bat	ball	squirrel	sailboat	sun
sofa	top	chair	dress	turtle
train	cat	telephone	apple	panda
dog	sandwich	orange	book	doll
bus	desk	glass	car	pear
snake	man	woman	plate	boot
bear	flower	spoon	suit	shoe
grapes	peaches	fork	rabbit	elephant
house	knife	lion	dolphin	fox
plum	horse	table	bee	mosquito

Words for Form B:

Toys	Furniture	Clothes
ball	chair	shirt
bicycle	table	pants
wagon	bed	ties
doll	stove	dress
game	couch	socks
stuffed animals	foot stool	sweater
train	bookshelf	hat
car	refrigerator	jacket
truck	rocking chair	blouse
jump rope	stool	shoes

(Materials list continues on page 38)

Fruit	Food	Transportation
apple	bread	bicycle
orange	milk	car
grape	cheese	feet
peach	eggs-omelet	bus
pear	lettuce	boat
strawberry	tomato	airplane
cherry	meat	train
banana	fruit	truck
grapefruit	pie	motorcycle
pineapple	cake	horse

Insects	Fish	Birds
bee	perch	cardinal
mosquito	trout	owl
grasshopper	eel	bobwhite
ant	black bass	robin
spider	catfish	tufted titmouse
butterfly	halibut	partridge
moth	mackerel	bluebird
caterpillar	sailfish	mallard
fly	tuna	condor
cricket	barracuda	green heron

Flowers	Animals	Weather
morning glory	collared peccary	moon
gladiolus	chipmunk	stars
iris	ferret	sun
zinnia	elk	snow
snapdragon	tiger	sky
camellia	monkey	wind
petunia	fox	clouds
poppy	elephant	rain
rose	rabbit	lightning
hollyhocks	wolf	rainbow

Professions	Vegatables
farmer	potato
nurse	peas
fireman	onion
policeman	celery
pilot	squash
bus driver	beet
dentist	cabbage
teacher	carrot
doctor	beans
mailman	lettuce

5) Large manila envelope (16x20-inches) for the materials.

PROCEDURE:
FORM A
1) Divide the students into two evenly matched teams.

2) Show the students the assorted word cards and picture cards.

3) Place the stacks face down on the table.

4) Students on each team arrange themselves in alphabetical order according to their first names. If students have the same first name, alphabetize by the first letter of last name. If more than one student's name has the same beginning letter, go to the second letter.

5) One student from each team tosses a die to determine who goes first. Student with the highest number goes first.

6) One student from the first team chooses a packet of word and object cards from the stacks that are face down on the table.

7) The student must place the words out on a table or the floor and then alphabetize the words and match the pictures with the words.

8) When all words are alphabetized and all pictures matched, the student raises a hand to indicate so; the teacher checks to see if the matching is correct.

9) If the words and pictures are correctly matched and alphabetized, the team receives five points; if not, the opposing team has a chance to alphabetize the words correctly and match the pictures. The second team then takes its regular turn.

10) Play continues in this manner until each student has had a chance to play.

FORM B
1) After students have played version A, display words and pictures in the following categories on tables: toys, furniture, clothes, fruit, food, transportation, insects, fish, birds, flowers, animals, weather, professions, and vegetables.

2) One student from the first team is asked to find names of toys beginning with B.

3) When a general category is given, such as furniture, students must alphabetize the list by the first letter and match each item with the correct picture.

4) When more than one picture has a name beginning with the letter called, the student alphabetizes by the second letter.

5) Five through ten are the same as in Form A.

■ ■ ■

PURPOSE: To train students to place letters in alphabetical order and to put together as many two and three letter words as possible.

GRADE LEVEL: Primary—1st and 2nd grades

TIME: 30 minutes

NUMBER: 16 students playing as individuals or paired

METHOD OF CHECKING: Teacher

MATERIALS:
1) Gooney Bird Letter Cards—number of cards will depend upon the number of students playing at any one time.

2) Vis-a-Vis® pen for each student.

3) Paper and pencils for each student.

4) Damp paper towels (to wipe the Vis-a-Vis® marker from the laminated Gooney Bird Card when finished).

5) Large manila envelope (12x15-inches) for the materials.

PROCEDURE:

1) Each player or pair of players is given a gooney bird card, a Vis-a-Vis® pen, a piece of paper, and a pencil.

2) The letters on the card are to be copied and arranged in alphabetical order on the bottom of the card.

3) Players, as they finish, raise a hand for the teacher to check the work.

4) If correct, the players begin to form as many two and three letter words as possible; on a separate piece of paper. If incorrect, the players continue work until the errors are corrected.

5) Correct alphabetical order on the first attempt scores two points; thereafter one point.

6) For each word correctly formed and placed in alphabetical order, the player or pair of players scores one point.

◄►◄►◄►◄►◄►◄►◄►◄►◄►◄►◄►◄►◄►◄►◄►◄►◄►◄►◄►
RACING LETTERS
◄►◄►◄►◄►◄►◄►◄►◄►◄►◄►◄►◄►◄►◄►◄►◄►◄►◄►◄►

PURPOSE: To give practice in alphabetizing letters.

GRADE LEVEL: Primary—1st and 2nd grades

TIME: Form A, 25 minutes. Form B, 25 minutes.

NUMBER: Best played with a maximum of 16 students

METHOD OF CHECKING: Teacher

MATERIALS:
1) 80 3x3-inch colored posterboard letter cards.

1) 16 6x9-inch manila envelopes, each containing 5 randomly chosen letters.

3) Large manila envelope (12x15-inches) for the materials.

PROCEDURE:
Form A
1) Divide the students into two evenly matched teams. A team captain is appointed by the teacher.

2) Each team lines up behind its respective team captain, facing each other from opposite sides of the room. Each team has a team table to work on.

3) Place Racing Letter envelopes, one for each team member, on the tables.

4) Each team captain chooses an envelope, lays the letters out on the table, and on signal from the teacher puts them in alphabetical order.

5) The teacher is at one team table and an older student or aide is at the other table to see that the letters are correctly alphabetized.

6) When a player is finished, the letters are placed back in the envelope, and he/she races to the opposite table with the envelope, places the envelope on the table, and races back to touch the next team member's hand to indicate "go."

7) Play continues in this fashion until all team members have taken a turn.

8) The first team to complete all envelopes correctly is the winner.
Form B
The same as Form A except two overhead projectors are used and the letters are written on 3x4-inch acetate sheets.
■ ■ ■

PURPOSE: To help students become more familiar with alphabetical order; specifically recognizing missing letters.

GRADE LEVEL: Primary—1st and 2nd grades

TIME: 25 minutes

NUMBER: Best played with a maximum of 16 students

METHOD OF CHECKING: Answer sheet

MATERIALS:
1) One 20x14-inch Express gameboard (see illustration on page 44) for each group of four students; number is determined by the number of players at any one time.
2) Four markers per gameboard.
3) One cloth sack to keep markers in per gameboard.
4) 120 3x3-inch colored posterboard cards (marked according to the list below), shuffled, and divided into four sets of 30 cards, one for each gameboard.

BCEF	MNPQ
LNOP	Take 2 turns
BDE	ABDE
SUVW	Go back 2 spaces
Move 1 space forward	GHIK
HIK	LMOP
EGHI	Take 2 turns
WYZ	ACD
QRTU	TUWX
Miss a turn	MNOP
OPQS	RSTV
EGHJ	Go back to start
CDF	DEGH
CEFG	Move 5 spaces forward
Long train, miss a turn	KMN
GHJK	RSUV
PQST	Go ahead 3 spaces
JKLN	NOPR
Go ahead 3 spaces	FGIJ
OQRS	Long train, miss a turn
JLMN	CEFG
HJKL	CDEG
Go to start	BDEF
NPQR	Miss a turn
Move 5 spaces forward	GIJK

(Materials list continues on page 45)

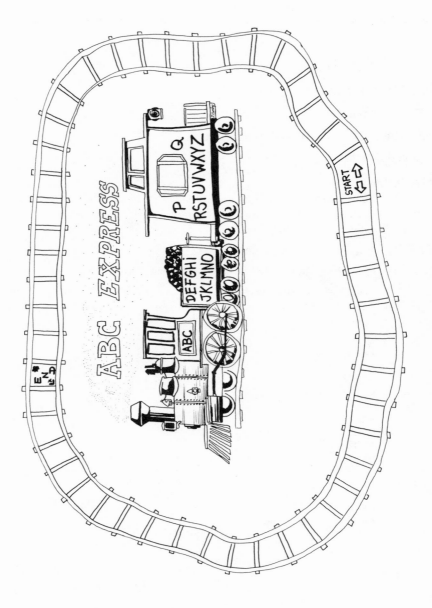

PRST
Move 1 space forward
JKMN
OPRS
JKMN
Go back 2 spaces
HIJL
NOQR
LNOP
Move ahead 1 space
BCDF
HIJL
Miss a turn
RTUV
JKMN
Long train, miss a turn
DFG
ABDE
Go ahead 3 spaces
UWXY
HJKL
Go back to start
TVW
IJKM
Take 2 turns
EFH
QSTU
Move 5 spaces forward
GHIK
VWY
Go back 2 spaces
FHI
STVW
OPQS
IJL

NPQR
PQST
SUVW
LNOP
Go back 2 spaces
DEG
JLMN
Move 5 spaces forward
VXYZ
RSUV
EGH
Take 2 turns
CDEG
UVXY
LMNP
Move ahead 1 space
QRSU
JKLM
Miss a turn
TUVX
FHIJ
XZ
Long train, miss a turn
GHJK
QRSU
Go ahead 3 spaces
HIK
PQRT
GIJK
Go back to start
STUW
ACD
IKLM
DEGH
NOQR

5) 4 answer sheets with the missing letters inserted, dry-mounted to a piece of colored posterboard.

6) Large manila envelope (16x20-inches) for the materials.

PROCEDURE:

1) Two-four players are to arrange themselves in alphabetical order, according to the first initials of their last names, around a table on which a gameboard has been placed. If two names begin with the same initial, second letter alphabetizing is required. The player whose name begins with the letter closest to the end of the alphabet starts.

(Procedures continue on page 46)

2) Players place markers at start and cards are in a pile face down on the board.

3) The first player draws a card and tells the letter that is missing.

4) If correct, the player moves the same number of spaces indicated on the card (each printed letter represents a space). If incorrect, he or she does not move, but may refer to the answer sheet.

5) The teacher should circulate among the tables to see that players are answering correctly and following directions on the cards.

6) Some cards are included that do not require an answer, but require the player to lose a turn, to move ahead, to go back, or to return to start. If a player draws one of these cards, the directions must be followed.

7) Players take turns (moving counter clockwise around the table) drawing cards, following directions and placing used cards in the discard pile.

8) The first player to reach the finish with the correct number of moves is the winner.

9) For an easier version, indicate the missing letter with a dash in the place where it belongs. (For example, CDE__G.)

■ ■ ■

PURPOSE: To develop facility in using the alphabet; particularly in recognizing a missing letter in a group of three to five letters.

GRADE LEVEL: Primary—3rd grade

TIME: 25 minutes

NUMBER: Best played with a maximum of 16 students

METHOD OF CHECKING: Teacher

MATERIALS:
1) Brown bag.
2) Treats or prizes; number to be determined by the number of players on any one team.
3) Timer.
4) 40 3x3-inch colored posterboard cards marked with the same letter combinations as found in ABC Express (see pages 43 and 45). This will be a more difficult version since there will be no alphabet available to look at.
5) Large manila envelope (10x13-inches) for the materials.

PROCEDURE:
1) Divide the students into two evenly matched teams.
2) Team captain arranges his/her players in a straight line in the order he/she thinks best suited for play.
3) Cards are placed face down on a table between the two teams.
4) A timer is set for 15 or 20 minutes.
5) The team whose captain's last name begins with the letter closest to the beginning of the alphabet starts.
6) The captain from team one draws a card, shows it to everyone, and tells the letter that is missing from the group of letters on the card. (Example: NPQR—letter O)
7) The teacher will indicate if the player is correct.
8) If correct, the card is placed in the discard pile and the player receives a brown bag with a treat or prize for everyone on the team. However, the bag is not opened until the end of the game.

(Procedures continue on page 48)

9) If the player is incorrect, the brown bag remains on the table by the cards and the card is placed at the bottom of the pile.

10) The captain from team two draws a card, shows it to everyone, and tells what letter is missing from his card.

11) If correct, the player on team two gets the bag from the player on team one or picks it up from the table. If incorrect, either the person from team one keeps the bag or it remains on the table.

12) This procedure continues until the timer rings.

13) The team that has the bag when the timer rings gets to share the treats or prizes. (The person who is holding the bag gets to draw out of the bag first and then holds the bag as the rest of the team draws a prize without looking.)

14) Each person who answers correctly, scores a point.

■ ■ ■

WORD-LETTER MATCHING

PURPOSE: To familiarize students with letters of the alphabet and the correct placement of letters to spell simple words.

GRADE LEVEL: Primary—1st grade

TIME: 25 minutes

NUMBER: Best played with a maximum of 16 students

METHOD OF CHECKING: Teacher

MATERIALS:
1) Two beanbags.
2) Two sets of 26 felt letters.
3) One gameboard of felt-covered cardboard, 36x36-inches (or whatever size is suitable).
   a) Divide the board into 6-inch squares with a black felt-tipped pen.
   b) In each square paste a picture of a familiar object, such as a dog, cat, man, woman and so on.
   c) Print the name of the object under the picture.
4) Large manila envelope (16x20-inches) for the materials.

PROCEDURE:
1) Before the students arrive, place the gameboard on the floor, mark a line for players to put their toes on, provide a beanbag, and scatter felt letters on a table. Make sure the felt letters exactly match the shape of the letters used in the game squares.
2) Divide the students into two evenly matched teams.
3) One team member is chosen captain by the teacher.
4) Other members of the team line up behind the captain according to alphabetical order of first name. In the event of two players having the same first name or beginning initial, alphabetize by the last name.
5) The teacher chooses a number from 1 to 10, in order to determine team order of play.
6) The team whose captain guesses (or comes closest to) the number that the teacher has written down goes first.

(Procedures continue on page 50)

7) The first player tosses a beanbag on the gameboard and looks carefully at the picture the beanbag lands on and at its name. He/she then goes to the table, picks up the correct felt alphabet letters and places them on the felt board, in proper sequence, to match the letters on the gameboard.

8) If the letters are placed correctly, the team receives two points and the student returns the letters to the table. If not, the opposing team has a chance to place the letters correctly. Then the second team takes its regular turn.

9) Play continues in this manner until every student has had a chance to play.

10) The game may be played one or more times depending upon class interest and need for letter identification and placement.

PURPOSE: To promote skill in alphabetizing by the first letter.

GRADE LEVEL: Primary—3rd grade

TIME: 25 minutes

NUMBER: Best played with a maximum of 16 students

METHOD OF CHECKING: Teacher

MATERIALS:

1) 16 sheets of colored posterboard (9x12-inches) bearing pictures of different types of stores (see below and pages 52-55).

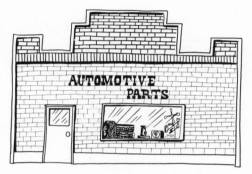

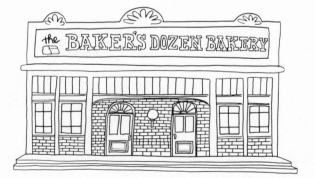

(Illustrations for Store Cards continue on page 52)

(Materials list continues on page 55)

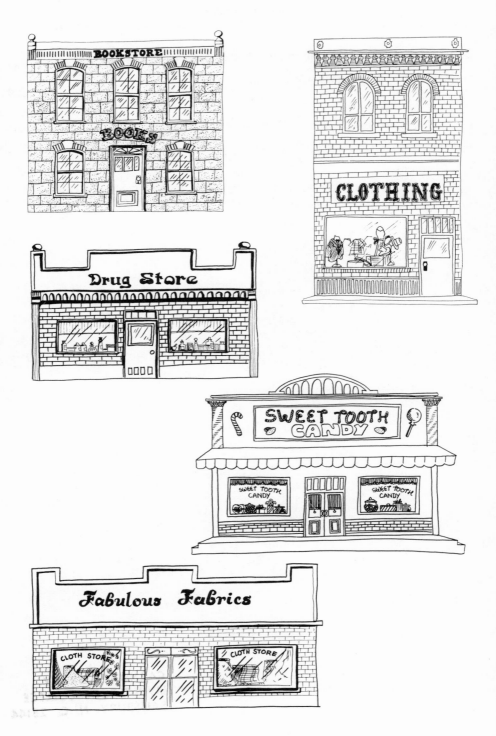

(Illustrations for Store Cards continue on page 54)

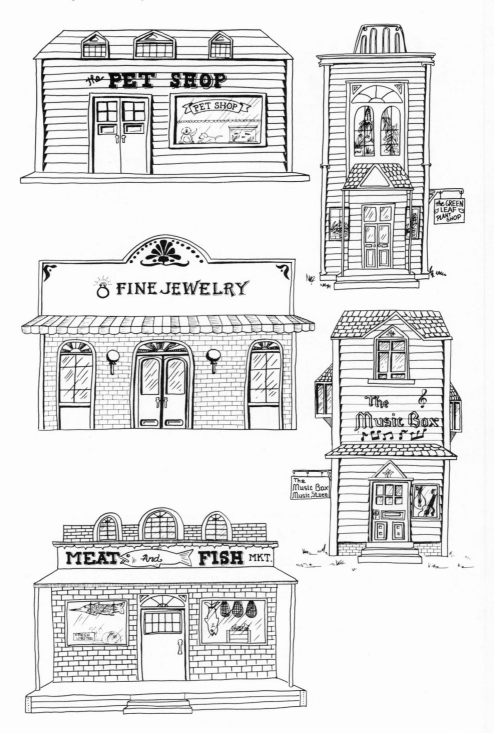

2) 6 tongue depressors for each store on which names of items found in that store are written. A total of 96 tongue depressors will be needed. Examples:

Automotive Store	**Bakery**	**Bookstore**	**Candy Shop**
tires	bread	cook book	jelly beans
oil	donuts	bookmark	chocolate
spark plugs	rolls	paperback book	nuts
battery	cakes	coloring book	lollipop
fuse	pies	children's book	sunflower seeds
jack	cookies	fiction	peanuts

(Materials list continues on page 56)

Clothing Store	Drug Store	Fabric Shop	Gift Shop
hat	curlers	thread	cards
skirt	hairbrush	needles	ashtray
blouse	lipstick	patterns	wrapping paper
coat	vitamins	scissors	music box
gloves	band-aids	cloth	ribbon
mittens	cough drops	buttons	candles

Grocery Store	Hardware Store	Jewelry Store	Healthfood Store
apple	nails	ring	vitamins
soup	hammer	bracelet	yogurt
milk	screwdriver	necklace	dried fruit
cookies	paint	pendant	banana chips
bread	ladder	pin	carob candy
butter	brush	watch	sesame seeds

Music Store	Pet Shop	Plant Store	Meat & Fish Market
trumpet	dog	rose bush	trout
oboe	cat	aloe cactus	lobster
guitar	bird	spider plant	salmon
trombone	leash	Swedish ivy	shrimp
flute	fish	wandering Jew	pork chops
drum	collars	English ivy	round steak

Record Store	Shoestore	Toy Store	Sporting Goods Store
jazz	boots	skateboard	basketball
disco	sandals	doll	football
classical	workshoes	game	T-shirt
country-western	tennis shoes	marbles	skis
rock	purses	jacks	tennis racquet
acid rock	house slippers	model airplane	baseball glove

3)   16 6x9-inch manila envelopes.

4)   Large manila envelope (16x20-inches) for the materials.

PROCEDURE:

1)   Each player is given a Store Card and envelope containing 6 tongue depressors.

2)   The player arranges the tongue depressors on the card in alphabetical order, raises a hand when finished, and has the teacher check to see if the depressors are correctly alphabetized.

3)   If correct, the player is given another card and begins again. If incorrect, the player re-arranges the tongue depressors to correct errors.

4)   Players score 10 points for each completed Shopping Card.

5)   The player with the most points wins.

■ ■ ■

▲►◄►◄►◄►◄►◄►◄►◄►◄►◄►◄►◄►◄►◄►◄►◄►◄►◄►
ALPHABET RACE
◄►◄►◄►◄►◄►◄►◄►◄►◄►◄►◄►◄►◄►◄►◄►◄►◄►◄►

PURPOSE: To give practice in alphabetizing skills from one-letter alphabetizing to four-letter alphabetizing.

GRADE LEVEL: 1st grade through 4th grade

TIME: 30 minutes

NUMBER: Best played with a maximum of 16 students

METHOD OF CHECKING: Teacher

MATERIALS:
1) Two dice.
2) 6x6-inch colored posterboard cards with words for alphabetizing—four packets for each of the following categories:

    a) Yellow packet indicates one-letter alphabetizing—three words = 1 point.

Novinger	Davis	Flack	Scott
Hartwell	Fideler	Evers	Moore
Slobodkin	Crabtree	Brown	Kipling

    b) Yellow packet indicates one-letter alphabetizing—six words = 3 points.

Bannon	Colby	Hurd	Townsend
Jones	Huber	Sharp	White
Hall	Koffler	Parker	Durbar
Sivords	Lenski	Tensen	Edge
Dickinson	Gipson	Lipkind	Shaar
Wolf	Martin	Dawson	Friskey

    c) Blue packet indicates two-letter alphabetizing—three words = 5 points.

today	than	stable	sense
tunnel	term	summer	speed
trip	tired	south	swallow

    d) Blue packet indicates two-letter alphabetizing—six words = 7 points.

during	music	animal	haphazard
distance	make	alphabet	hearse
destroy	metal	agree	hunter
dark	mystic	appoint	hinder
door	minute	assume	hoecake
dwell	move	azure	hyphen

(Materials list continues on page 58)

e)   Red packet indicates three-letter alphabetizing — three words =
     9 points.

cab	captain	caller	cad
calf	card	camp	camera
cape	cage	cable	cap

f)   Red packet indicates three-letter alphabetizing — six words = 11
     points.

canal	cement	each	key
camel	cedar	eaglet	kelp
call	cellar	eardrum	keel
cake	censor	easily	kerchief
cabin	ceiling	eatable	keg
catfish	certain	eaves	kettle

g)   Orange packet indicates four-letter alphabetizing — three words
     = 13 points.

merit	profit	honk	wheel
mere	procedure	honest	where
mercy	property	honor	whet

h)   Orange packet indicates four-letter alphabetizing — six words =
     15 points.

percent	wordless	scold	gargle
perfect	worker	scoff	garish
period	wore	scone	garlic
permit	world	scoop	garnet
perk	worse	score	garter
persist	wormwood	scotch	garret

3)   Large manila envelope (16x20-inches) for the materials.

PROCEDURE:

1)   The students are evenly divided into two teams.

2)   One die is provided to each team captain who then rolls the die for a
     number. The team with the highest number gets the first turn.

3)   Packets of cards are arranged by difficulty and are worth more or
     fewer points, depending on difficulty.

4)   One student from the first team (chosen by the captain) selects a
     packet of cards from a category and places the words in alphabetical
     order. (Use chalkboard rail, flannel board or floor.)

5)   If the words are in correct alphabetical order, the team receives the
     points; if not, the opposing team has a chance to alphabetize them
     correctly. It then takes its regular turn.

6)   Team captains will choose which team members will alphabetize
     until everyone has had a turn.

7)   The team with the most points wins.

■ ■ ■

▲▶ ▲▶ ▲▶ ▲▶ ▲▶ ▲▶ ▲▶ ▲▶ ▲▶ ▲▶ ▲▶ ▲▶ ▲▶ ▲▶ ▲▶ ▲▶ ▲▶ ▲▶ ▲▶

THE MATCHING GAME

▲▶ ▲▶ ▲▶ ▲▶ ▲▶ ▲▶ ▲▶ ▲▶ ▲▶ ▲▶ ▲▶ ▲▶ ▲▶ ▲▶ ▲▶ ▲▶ ▲▶ ▲▶ ▲▶

PURPOSE: To give practice in alphabetizing by first letters.

GRADE LEVEL: 3rd and 4th grades

TIME: 25 minutes

NUMBER: Best played with a maximum of 16 students

METHOD OF CHECKING: Teacher

MATERIALS:

1) 80 3x3-inch colored posterboard cards with categories listed below (some may be duplicated):

a vehicle	a number	a favorite food
a tool	a flower	a game
a toy	a girl's name	a boy's name
a car	an author	a part of the body
a soup	a color	a tree
an animal	a river	a musical instrument
a bird	a fish	a fruit
a state	a coin	a piece of clothing
an insect	a dog	something in a kitchen
a country	a sport	a piece of furniture
a vegetable	the name of a president	a farm animal
a planet	a magazine	an ice cream flavor
the name of a street	a house plant	a month of the year
a day of the week	a favorite TV program	something cool to drink

2) 80 strips of scrap paper approximately 2x3-inches.

3) Optional—dictionaries for each student.

4) Large manila envelope (12x15-inches) for the materials.

PROCEDURE:

1) Students count off in fours and divide into four groups.

2) Each student is given five strips of scrap paper and five 3x3-inch match cards.

(Procedures continue on page 60)

3) The player lists one item for each match card on the scrap paper. For example:

a game — tic-tac-toe
a toy — ball
a number — five
a color — red
a bird — robin

Students may use dictionaries for ideas or spelling.

4) When the five cards are completed, the student alphabetizes the slips of paper. For example:

ball — a toy
five — a number
red — a color
robin — a bird
tic-tac-toe — a game

5) When a player is finished and raises a hand to indicate so, the teacher checks the cards and slips.

6) If correct, the player receives five points, turns over the slips of paper, and is given five different match cards to complete in the same manner for an additional five points.

7) If incorrect, the player continues work until all five cards are correctly alphabetized and then procedes as in Step 6.

■ ■ ■

PIC-A-LETTER

PURPOSE: To encourage students to enjoy working with letters.

GRADE LEVEL: Intermediate — 3rd and 4th grades

TIME: 15 minutes

NUMBER: Best played with a maximum of 16 students

METHOD OF CHECKING: Teacher

MATERIALS:
1) 16 Pic-A-Letter boards of 9x12-inch oak-tag.

Pic-A-Letter

1. a vegetable . . . . P
2. a beverage . . . . T
3. body of water L
4. question . . . . Y
5. exclamation . . . . O, G
6. female sheep . . . . U
7. insect . . . . B
8. girl's name . . . . D, B, K
9. golf term . . . . T
10. part of the face I
11. what eyes do C
12. line of people . . . . Q
13. not me . . . . U
14. bird . . . . J

---

2) 16 6x9-inch manila envelopes containing slips of paper upon which are written assorted letters of the alphabet. Include duplicate letters.

(Materials list continues on page 62)

3) Master sheet of definitions and letters dry-mounted to a piece of colored posterboard.

4) Large manila envelope (12x15-inches) for the materials.

PROCEDURE:

1) Each player is given a Pic-A-Letter board and envelope containing letters.

2) The player matches the definition with the letter that sounds like the word. When finished the player raises a hand to indicate so, and the teacher checks the board.

3) The players receive one point for each correct match.

4) The player who finishes first, wins. If no player finishes, the player with the most points wins.

AUTHOR SCRAMBLE

PURPOSE: To adapt alphabetizing skills from one-letter alphabetizing to two-letter alphabetizing.

GRADE LEVEL: Intermediate—4th grade

TIME: 25 minutes

NUMBER: Best played with a maximum of 16 students

METHOD OF CHECKING: Teacher

MATERIALS:

1) 4 sets of 4x8-inch colored posterboard labels with authors' names printed in black felt tip pen and with a hole punched at each end. 16 cards per set for a total of 64 cards.

Set I	Set II	Set III	Set IV
Aardema, Verna	Adrian, Mary	Aliki	Augelli, John
Aesop	Caney, Steven	Dickens, Charles	Barth, Edna
Baker, Eugene	Carroll, Lewis	Eckert, Allan	Bliven, Bruce
Farber, Norma	Folsom, Franklin	Erdoes, Richard	Del Rey, Lester
Hamilton, Virginia	Hawes, Judy	Gag, Wanda	Enright, Elizabeth
Jackson, Shirley	Joslin, Sesyle	Inouye, Carol	Gurney, Gene
Kastner, Erich	Kingman, Lee	Lampman, Evelyn	Ingrams, Doreen
Madison, Arnold	May, Julian	Moody, Ralph	Ish-Kishor, Sulamith
McGowen, Tom	Milgrom, Harry	Neurath, Marie	Jordan, June
Oliver, John	Orton, Helen	Nourse, Alan	Lear, Edward
Renick, Marion	Ricciuti, Edward	Parks, Aileen	Naden, Corinne
Sasek, Miroslav	Simon, Norma	Quackenbush, Robert	Nyce, Vera
Urquhart, David	Vermeer, Jackie	Taylor, Theodore	Podendorf, Illa
Walsh, John	Warburg, Sandol	Webster, David	Taber, Gladys
Wilson, Charles	Wohlrobe, Raymond	Yolen, Jane	Unkelbach, Kurt
Zaffo, George	Zappler, Georg	Yaroslavia	Wyler, Rose

2) String or yarn to put through the tops of the author labels.

3) Large manila envelope (12x15-inches) for the materials.

PROCEDURE:

1) Divide the students into two evenly matched teams. Team captains are chosen.

2) Author labels, by set, are placed face down on a table, around which students are gathered.

3) Each student chooses an author label, hangs it around his/her neck, and goes over to the team captains.

(Procedures continue on page 64)

4) Once all students are gathered around the team captain, the teacher shouts "go" and team members must place themselves in alphabetical order according to the author's last name.

5) When the author labels are alphabetized, the team captain calls the teacher over to check the team's work. If the team is correct, it chooses a second set and proceeds in the same manner.

6) If the order is not correct, the team is questioned as to why members placed themselves in that order. The questioning should continue until all names are correctly alphabetized.

7) The first team to alphabetize all authors correctly wins the game.

8) If more practice is needed, start the procedure over using a different set of author cards.

■ ■ ■

TWADDLE

PURPOSE: To give practice in alphabetizing words and to have fun.

GRADE LEVEL: Intermediate—4th and 5th grades

TIME: 25 minutes

NUMBER: Best played with a maximum of 16 students

METHOD OF CHECKING: Self-checking

MATERIALS:

1) 1 overhead projector.

2) 1 screen.

3) 32 6x9-inch manila envelopes with riddles written on the outside. The answers to these riddles must be made up of words that are in alphabetical order. Each word of each answer is written on a separate piece of 1x3-inch acetate paper, and all of the pieces are placed in the envelope. For example:

> Do you know how long waddling Walruses can be caged? (Just like short waddling Walruses.)
>
> What kind of coat has no buttons or zipper? (A coat of paint.)
>
> What does the Jolly Green Giant do? (He hoe hoe hoes.)
>
> What fishes' ears are the farthest apart? (All biggest fish.)
>
> What is worse than finding two wriggling worms in your salad? (Finding halves of two wriggling worms.)

4) 1 die.

5) Large manila envelope (16x20-inches) for the materials.

PROCEDURE:

1) Two teams are formed by counting off in twos. Captains are chosen by the teacher.

2) Each team lines up seated behind the captain facing the screen.

3) The captains roll the die to determine the order of play.

4) The first player receives an envelope from the teacher, reads the riddle aloud and empties the acetate slips on the overhead projector.

5) If the words on the slips are alphabetized correctly, the answer to the riddle is given.

(Procedures continue on page 66)

6) The player has one minute to alphabetize the words in order to get the answer.

7) If correct, 5 points are scored for the team and the other team takes a turn. If incorrect, the opposing team can score 5 points by alphabetizing the words correctly. It then takes its regular turn.

8) Play continues with teams alternating turns.

9) The team with the most points wins.

CATEGORIES

PURPOSE: To give practice in alphabetizing by first, second, and third letter.

GRADE LEVEL: 3rd grade through 6th grade

TIME: 25 minutes

NUMBER: Best played with a maximum of 16 students

METHOD OF CHECKING: Teacher

MATERIALS:
1) 16 Category boards made out of 9x12-inch oak-tag. For best results use different boards for each student.

VEHICLES	TOOLS	FARM ANIMALS

2) 16 sets of 1x3-inch cards made from colored posterboard with one word written on each card (21 cards in a set). The sets below are suggested categories and word lists:

SET I

Vehicles	Tools	Farm Animals
car	hammer	chicken
truck	saw	duck
bus	chisel	cow
van	screwdriver	horse
motorcycle	wrench	sheep
bicycle	ax	pig
tractor	vise	goose

(Materials list continues on page 68)

SET II

Animals	Birds	Clothes
giraffe	cardinal	coat
deer	blue jay	vest
elephant	grackle	trousers
rhinoceros	crow	dress
penguin	robin	jacket
gorilla	wren	blouse
zebra	bluebird	sweater

SET III

Toys	Girls' Names	Months
ball	Carol	December
bat	Sue	March
top	Mary	June
doll	Angela	August
marbles	Debra	February
jacks	Theresa	May
rattle	Juanita	September

SET IV

Sports	Cars	Insects
baseball	Ford	beetles
football	Chevrolet	ant
soccer	Pontiac	fly
track	Volkswagon	bee
swimming	Mercury	hornet
tennis	Lincoln	wasp
hockey	Chrysler	caterpillar

SET V

Parts of the Body	Flowers	Boys' Names
foot	rose	Paul
hand	daisy	Joseph
finger	lilly	William
eye	buttercup	Steven
toe	marigold	Manuel
knee	lilac	Alfred
elbow	peony	Thomas

SET VI

States	Countries	Numbers
Colorado	United States	one
Massachusetts	Germany	seven
Illinois	Japan	eight
Washington	Egypt	ten
New York	England	nine
Arizona	Norway	five
New Mexico	Sweden	two

SET VII

Reptiles	Trees	Fruit
snakes	blue spruce	apple
alligators	pine	orange
crocodiles	oak	pear
lizards	maple	peach
toads	elm	cherry
frogs	cottonwood	grape
salamander	olive	banana

SET VIII

Streets	Kitchen Things	Uniforms
Colfax	stove	policeman
Main	refrigerator	fireman
Federal	cabinets	Air Force
Speer	food	Coast Guard
Broadway	toaster	nurse
Lowell	mixer	Army
Fifth Avenue	pans	Navy

SET IX

Food	Vegetables	Ice Cream
chicken	carrot	chocolate
pizza	pinto bean	vanilla
taco	green bean	banana
steak	celery	strawberry
roast beef	pepper	butterscotch
hamburger	corn	peach
spaghetti	squash	neopolitan

SET X

Beverages	Soups	Games
Coke	vegetable	chess
Pepsi	mushroom	checkers
orange	chicken noodle	Monopoly
root beer	clam chowder	dominoes
Bubble-up	onion	hop scotch
Seven-up	bean	hide-and-seek
lemonade	split pea	jump rope

SET XI

Mammals	Dogs	Cats
rabbit	collie	Persian
man	German shepherd	calico
deer	poodle	Siamese
antelope	Irish setter	Burmese
moose	pug	manx
monkey	boxer	angora
giraffe	St. Bernard	tabby

(Materials list continues on page 70)

SET XII

Types of Books	Furniture	Musical Instruments
fantasy	chair	piano
science fiction	table	drum
historical fiction	sofa	clarinet
biography	dresser	tuba
fairy tales	desk	violin
mystery	bookcase	trumpet
adventure	bed	fiddle

SET XIII

Authors	Adjectives	Colors
Rey, Margaret	pretty	yellow
Alexander, Lloyd	sad	white
Sewell, Anna	little	purple
Cooper, Susan	big	green
Sendak, Maurice	happy	blue
Showers, Paul	poor	magenta
Bond, Michael	rich	orange

SET XIV

Rivers	Presidents	Transportation
Colorado	Ford, Gerald	bus
Mississippi	Johnson, Andrew	automobile
Green	Lincoln, Abraham	train
Platte	Washington, George	airplane
Missouri	Eisenhower, Dwight	motorcycle
Yukon	Kennedy, John	bicycle
Susquehanna	Adams, John	moped

SET XV

Continents	Fish	Minerals
North America	trout	iron
South America	cod	calcite
Europe	shark	agate
Asia	goldfish	pyrite
Africa	salmon	topaz
Anarctica	haddock	quartz
Australia	sardine	diamond

SET XVI

Money	Planets	House Plants
penny	Mercury	rubber plant
dime	Mars	spider plant
quarter	Pluto	cactus
half-dollar	Venus	Swedish ivy
nickel	Jupiter	shamrock
silver dollar	Earth	geranium
dollar	Neptune	aloe vera

3) 16 6x9-inch envelopes for the category cards; labeled on the outside.

4) Large manila envelope (16x20-inches) for the materials.

PROCEDURE:
1) Each student is given a Category board.

2) The student removes the cards from the envelope fastened to the back of the board and alphabetizes each set under the proper category.

3) When a player is finished and raises a hand to indicate so, the teacher checks to see if the board is alphabetized and categorized correctly.

4) If correct, the student scores 21 points and may choose a center or if more practice is needed, the student may trade boards with someone else.

5) If incorrect, the player continues work until all cards are correctly categorized and alphabetized, and then proceeds as in Step 4.

■ ■ ■

ALPHA-RIDDLE QUIZ

PURPOSE: To provide practice in verbalizing or writing the alphabet, and to promote the ability to name a word beginning with a particular letter and to make up a riddle about the letter.

GRADE LEVEL: 3rd and 4th grades

TIME: Form A—25 minutes; Form B—25 minutes

NUMBER: Best played with a maximum of 16 students

METHOD OF CHECKING: Teacher

MATERIALS:
1) "Riddle" ditto sheets printed on oak-tag paper for the students to answer and to unscramble into alphabetical order. The following is a suggested list; scramble them when writing them for students.

A—season of the year	N—something used in sewing
B—sport	O—bird
C—pet	P—cooking utensil
D—place where butter is made	Q—coin
E—something to eat	R—flower
F—pretty plant	S—fish
G—fuel	T—part of your body
H—tool	U—country of the world
I—state of the U.S.	V—flavor of ice cream
J—month of the year	W—something cool to drink
K—animal	X—musical instrument
L—body of water	Y—something used in knitting
M—delicious drink	Z—substitute for button

2) Large manila envelope (10x13-inches) for the materials.

PROCEDURE:
FORM A
1) Students sit in a circle with the teacher.

2) The teacher starts the game by beginning with the letter A and a riddle (season of the year).

3) The player to the right answers with the correct word (autumn) or forfeits the chance to score a point. If the answer is incorrect, anyone in the circle may answer and score a point.

4) Play resumes with the student who correctly answered the riddle posing another riddle, with the next letter, to the player on the right.

5) Play continues until all letters are used or time is called.

6) One point is scored for each correct answer. The student with the most number of points, at the end, is the winner.

FORM B

1) Hand out a "riddle" ditto sheet to each student.

2) Students are to answer the riddles and then place the answers in correct alphabetical order on a separate sheet of paper.

■ ■ ■

PURPOSE: To promote skill in alphabetizing by using authors' last names.

GRADE LEVEL: Intermediate — 5th and 6th grades

TIME: Part I — 50 minutes; Part II — 50 minutes

NUMBER: Best played with a maximum of 16 players

METHOD OF CHECKING: Teacher

MATERIALS:
1) Chalkboard and chalk.

2) Ditto sheet of alphabet letters.

3) For Part II — three colored strips (colored posterboard or paint chips) for each student.

PROCEDURE:
PART I
1) Divide the students into two evenly matched teams. Each team is to pick a captain.

2) Hand each team captain a dittoed list of the alphabet. Write the letters on a chalkboard.

3) Allow ten minutes to see how many letters of the alphabet a team can name an author for. More than one author's name may be placed next to a letter; the more the better.

4) During this time players may walk around the room recording as many names as possible as long as they are all, in the end, recorded on the master list in alphabetical order.

5) Allow students to study the list for a few minutes; then collect it.

6) The team whose captain's last name begins with the initial closest to the beginning of the alphabet starts.

7) From memory, starting with the letter A, team one gives an author whose name begins with that letter. If correct, the team scores a point, and play passes on to team two who must provide a name for the next letter. If incorrect, play passes on to team two who takes that turn as well as the turn for the next letter. The teacher, meanwhile, is recording the names on the chalkboard.

8) Play continues in this fashion until all the letters are used up or until time runs out. In the latter instance, resume play, next time, with the last letter used.

9) The team that has scored the most points for the correct answers is the winner.

PART II

1) Players gather around a "team table."

2) Hand each team captain the team's list plus the list recorded on the chalkboard.

3) The team captain is to assign, at least, three authors' names to each player who must then go to the shelves and find a book written by that author.

4) When the book has been located, a colored strip is inserted in the space. The book is brought to the "team table" and placed in a stack.

5) When all three books have been found by a player, that player is to call the teacher for checking. Once the books are checked, they are re-shelved in the proper place.

6) If a book cannot be located, the player is to show the teacher where it belongs on the shelves.

7) For each book found and re-shelved correctly, the player scores two points. Colored strips are left in place so that the teacher may check to see if the book is re-shelved correctly.

PURPOSE: To provide practice in alphabetizing skills from two-letter alphabetizing to four-letter alphabetizing.

GRADE LEVEL: Intermediate—4th grade

TIME: 25 minutes

NUMBER: Best played with a maximum of 16 students

METHOD OF CHECKING: Teacher

MATERIALS:
1) 16 Alpha Stands—can be the tops of styrofoam egg cartons with five slots cut into the tops. Slots are approximately two inches long.

2) 2x2-inch colored posterboard cards on which are printed the words to be used. Number the backs of cards (1-64). Number will depend upon the number of students playing at any one time. Plan on five cards per envelope and a total of four envelopes per player (20 cards per student). A total of 320 cards will be needed (based on 16 students). The following are suggested sets of words:

slate	disc	pony	border	sight	sled
sky	ditch	polo	boost	sling	sleep
skirt	dip	poncho	bonnet	slip	sleet
slam	dirty	point	body	slit	slept
slit	dive	poet	bone	sing	slick
poke	bomb	actor	cake	each	over
poll	boon	acre	caird	eager	oyster
pop	bottle	abuse	cadre	earth	owe
plug	boy	absorb	cedar	echo	obtain
plus	bow	action	chant	eclair	oblong

3) 64 6x9-inch manila envelopes to keep the word cards in, numbered on the outside to correspond to the numbers on the back of the cards.

4) Store envelopes in an appropriately sized cardboard box or in a large manila envelope (16x20-inches).

PROCEDURE:
1) Each player is given an Alpha Stand and an envelope.

2) Each player is to remove the cards from the envelope, study them and then alphabetize them.

3) Place the alphabetized cards in the slots on the Alpha Stand.

4) When finished, players raise hands and the teacher checks to see if they are correctly alphabetized.

5) If correct, the cards are returned to the envelope and a new envelope is chosen. Play continues in the same fashion until a player has completed four envelopes. When four have been completed, the player may help someone who is having trouble.

6) If incorrect, work continues until all five cards are correctly alphabetized. When finished, the player files the cards back in an envelope and a new one is taken.

7) Each player receives a point for each word in the correct slot for a total of five points per envelope.

8) The player with the most points, at the end of the period, wins.

■ ■ ■

THUMBS

PURPOSE: To promote skill and speed in determining if words are alphabetized correctly.

GRADE LEVEL: Intermediate—5th and 6th grades

TIME: 20 minutes

NUMBER: Best played with a maximum of 16 students

METHOD OF CHECKING: Teacher

MATERIALS:
1) 35 sheets of 9x12-inch oak-tag bearing 3 to 5 words. (Words should be large enough to be read when held up in front of the group.) I or C is placed on the reverse side to indicate to the teacher if the words are alphabetized correctly or incorrectly. A few examples are:

gossamer	centre	roller	menthol
gossan	centrifugal	rollback	mentor
gossip	centrosome	rollbook	mention
		rolling mill	
		rollicking	

2) Chalkboard, chalk and eraser.

3) Large manila envelope (12x15-inches) for the materials.

PROCEDURE:
1) Two teams are formed by counting off in twos and the teacher chooses a captain for each team.

2) The captains do not play the game but act as scorekeepers at the chalkboard.

3) The teams form two lines in front of the captains facing the chalkboard.

4) The teacher sits between the lines facing the teams and shows a card to team one.

5) Each member of the team responds with a thumb-up if the words are correctly alphabetized or with a thumb-down if the words are incorrectly alphabetized. 15 seconds is given before a count of the correct responses is taken, when the teacher indicates the correct answer.

6) The number of correct thumb responses is the team score for that round.

7) Team two is shown a card and follows the same procedure.

8) Play continues with teams alternating turns.

9) After 15 minutes of play, the team with the highest score wins.

CRACKER JACK

PURPOSE: To promote accuracy and speed in alphabetizing abbreviations.

GRADE LEVEL: Intermediate—5th and 6th grades

TIME: 25 minutes

NUMBER: Best played with a maximum of 16 students

METHOD OF CHECKING: Teacher

MATERIALS:

1) 60 2x2-inch colored posterboard cards on which are printed two abbreviations.

CO	CA	cen.	lang.	temp.	teleg.
IN	Mr.	amp.	bgs.	Unesco	WASP
MA	MS	Cant.	Cath.	St.	SIB
MD	NE	CBS	indef.	ry.	Rom.
KS	KY	Gk.	Gal.	jour.	impf.
AL	AZ	astr.	Bapt.	Geo.	gals.
NY	ND	fid.	diff.	comp.	fin.
WA	WI	coll.	litho.	elec.	dyn.
IL	IA	mtge.	med.	freq.	mtg.
SD	SC	Ra.	prob.	mfg.	ldg.
Mrs.	OR	nom.	orch.	Ire.	Geog.
VA	FL	myst.	yld.	conj.	fz.
chem.	bio.	univ.	mis.	abr.	anc.
Inc.	hdqrs.	MSS	Sen.	Braz.	avg.
guar.	impv.	Rus.	TASS	ave.	fed.
AK	amb.	USSR	VAT	exch.	dept.
agric.	cap.	Xmas	WY	cyl.	div.
Feb.	Jan.	Apr.	Dec.	Nov.	Oct.
Sept.	Aug.	Jl.	Je.	My.	Mar.
UT	OK	WV	TX	MO	GA

2) Two dice.

3) Large manila envelope (10x13-inches) for the materials.

PROCEDURE:

1) Divide the students into two evenly matched teams.

2) Players are to arrange themselves in alphabetical order according to the first initial of last name, behind the team captain. If two names begin with the same initial, second letter alphabetizing is required.

3) One die is provided to each team captain who then throws the die for a number. The team with the highest number gets the first turn.

(Procedures continue on page 80)

4) The first player from team one chooses a card and reads the two words on the card.

5) The player states which abbreviated word would come first and the reason why it belongs first.

6) If correct, the team keeps the card and play passes on to the next team. If incorrect, the card is placed at the bottom of the pile; play passes on to the next team who, if they correctly alphabetize the first time, receive an extra turn.

7) The team with the most cards at the end of play is the CRACKER JACKS!

8) One point is scored for each abbreviation card correctly alphabetized.

■ ■ ■

PURPOSE: To provide practice in recognizing letter-by-letter and word-by-word alphabetizing.

GRADE LEVEL: Intermediate—5th and 6th grades

TIME: 30 minutes

NUMBER: Best played with a maximum of 16 students

METHOD OF CHECKING: Answer sheet

MATERIALS:

    1) 4 Lickety-Split gameboards made of colored posterboard (16x22-inches).

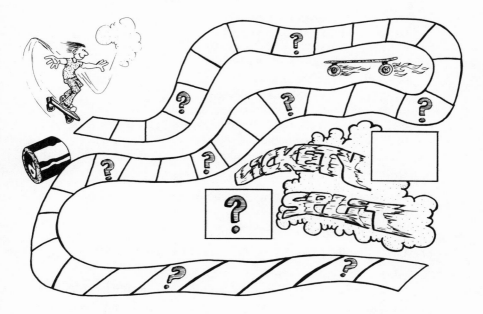

    2)   4 sets of 25 3x4-inch colored posterboard Lickety-Split cards bearing words alphabetized word-by-word or letter-by-letter. A total of 100 cards will be needed. For example:

Letter-by-letter

air cargo	air carrier	air cell
air alert	air attack	air base
air bed	air bladder	airborne
anchor man	anchor plant	anchor pocket
monkey	monkey business	monkey shine

Word-by-word

air brake	air lock	airedale
horse	horsemanship	horses
air transport	air war	aircraft
Ibo	in came Pinky	Inca Indians
Hall of Mirrors	Halladay	Houdini

3) 4 answer sheets dry-mounted to a piece of colored posterboard.

4) 4 sets of 10 3x4-inch colored posterboard ? cards bearing specific directions (a total of 40 cards will be needed):

crack in the sidewalk—move back 2 spaces
tail wind—move ahead 2 spaces
hit a small rock—lose one turn
head winds—move back 1 space
nice going, take another turn
bumpy cement—go back 2 spaces
going downhill—move ahead 3 spaces
lucky card, roll the die and move ahead that many spaces
bad luck, roll the die and move back that many spaces
good luck, move double the number rolled on the die

5) 4 dice.

6) 16 markers, 4 for each gameboard (miniature skateboards, if possible).

7) 4 cloth bags or letter size envelopes.

8) Large manila envelope (16x20-inches) for the materials.

PROCEDURE:

1) Groups of four are formed by counting off in fours.

2) Each group is given a Lickety-split gameboard and related materials, and arranges itself around the gameboard on the floor.

3) The Lickety-Split cards and ? cards are placed face down in a pile on the designated places on the gameboard. All markers are placed at start, and one die is rolled to determine the order of play.

4) The first player rolls a die, draws a Lickety-Split card, and identifies the alphabetizing as word-by-word or letter-by-letter. The other players may check the answer sheet, if in doubt.

5) If correct, the player moves the number of spaces as indicated on the die and places the card at the bottom of the pile. If incorrect, the next player takes a turn.

6) If a player lands on a space with a ?, a ? card is drawn, the directions are followed, and the card is placed at the bottom of the pile.

7) Play continues in this manner with players alternating turns.

8) The first player to reach the finish wins.

PURPOSE: To familiarize students with authors' names.

GRADE LEVEL: Intermediate—5th and 6th grades

TIME: Part I—50 minutes; Part II—25 minutes

NUMBER: Best played with a maximum of 16 students

METHOD OF CHECKING: Teacher

MATERIALS:
1) 1 oak-tag author sheet bearing a list of authors' names for each student. There should be a book on the shelves for each author on the list.

2) Pencils and paper for each student.

3) Between two and five colored strips (colored posterboard or paint chips) for each student.

4) Master sheet dry-mounted to a piece of colored posterboard. The list should be composed of the list of authors that was given to the students and clues to the identity of each author composed so that the first letter of each word in the clue matches the author's initials. The following are a few examples:

Weird imagination	Washington Irving
Clever delineator	Charles Dickens
Heroism wisely lauded	Henry Wadsworth Longfellow
Little Massachusetts author	Louisa May Alcott
Life in Wisconsin	Laura Ingalls Wilder
Author noted	Andre Norton
Jolly George fathead	Jean Guttery Fritz
Curley, Scrumble, Knoll	Carol Seegar Kendall
Gods, elves, heroes	Gail Einhart Haley

5) Large manila envelope (12x15-inches) for the materials.

PROCEDURE:
PART I
1) Students are to sit in a circle with the teacher. Places are determined by alphabetizing according to the first initials of the students' first names. If there is duplication of letters, go to the second letters of the first names.

2) Each student is given a 6x9-inch oak-tag sheet with the authors' complete names.

3) The teacher is to read off the master list the words used to indicate the author's name. (Example: Weird imagination)

4) Players look at their oak-tag sheets to find the name which fits the description (Washington Irving).

5) The player to the teacher's right must answer with the correct author or forfeit the chance to score a point. If the answer is incorrect, anyone in the circle may answer, thus scoring a point. Play resumes with the next student answering the teacher's word hints.

6) Players are to mark, on a piece of paper, the names they guess correctly.

7) Play continues until all names are used or time runs out. In the latter instance, pick up next time with the last name used.

8) When all names have been guessed, the players are to alphabetize them according to the way they would be found upon the shelves.

9) One point is scored for each correctly guessed answer and two points for the correct alphabetizing of authors' names.

PART II

1) After Part I has been completed, each player goes to the shelves to find the book bearing the name of each author he/she identified correctly.

2) When the book is found, a colored strip is inserted in the space. The book is brought to the teacher for checking and then returned to the shelves. If a book cannot be found, the player is to show the teacher where it belongs on the shelves.

3) For each book found and re-shelved correctly, the player scores two points. Colored strips are left in place so that the teacher may check to see if the book is re-shelved correctly.

PART II – DR. JOHNSON'S LEGACY:
The Dictionary

A dictionary is a book that contains a selected list of words arranged in alphabetical order. It may also give the origin and pronunciation of each word and may quote passages from speeches and works of literature to illustrate its use. Some dictionaries include rules of grammar and spelling and lists of proper names and of abbreviations.

Before a student uses a dictionary, he should become familiar with the methods, principles and scope of the book. All good dictionaries today have introductory sections that explain what the book contains and how the dictionary is arranged.

The first thing a dictionary entry shows is how to spell a word and how to divide it into syllables. Accent marks and symbols that are explained in the book tell a student how to pronounce the word. Many dictionaries also tell what part of speech the word is. Definitions of the word usually follow. Most dictionaries use the word in a sentence or quotation to help define it. Sometimes they add pictures or drawings to tell more about the entry.

After the definitions, many dictionaries include a list of synonyms, or words having about the same meaning as the word being defined. Sometimes a list of antonyms (words with opposite meanings) follows the synonyms.

The games within this chapter are designed to familiarize students with the many and varied uses of a dictionary. The following audiovisual materials would be a good way to spark discussion.

What's in the Dictionary? [Filmstrip]. Using the Elementary School Library. Chicago, Society for Visual Education, Inc. Sound, 16 minutes, color.

Getting Acquainted with Sources of Information: The Dictionary [Audio cassette]. How to Use the Library. Tulsa, OK, Educational Progress Corporation. (Tape 8, Part I, and Tape 9, Part II; 20 minutes each tape).

How to Use the Dictionary [Filmstrip]. School Library Series. New York, McGraw-Hill. Part I, 36 fr.; Part II, 45 fr.; color.

Dictionary Skills. Developed and edited by Roberta LaCoste. Ideal. 18 charts, color.

Your Dictionary and How to Use It [Filmstrip]. First You Find It; Then Define It Series. Chicago, Society for Visual Education. 26 fr., color.

Who's Mispronouncing [Filmstrip]. Your Dictionary and How to Use It. Chicago, Society for Visual Education. 34 fr., color.

Words and Their Ways [Filmstrip]. Your Dictionary and How to Use It. Chicago, Society for Visual Education. 28 fr., color.

You Can Find Words Easily [Filmstrip]. Your Dictionary and How to Use It. Chicago, Society for Visual Education. 27 fr., color.

◄► ◄► ◄► ◄► ◄► ◄► ◄► ◄► ◄► ◄► ◄► ◄► ◄► ◄► ◄► ◄► ◄► ◄► ◄►
GUIDE WORD MATCH
◄► ◄► ◄► ◄► ◄► ◄► ◄► ◄► ◄► ◄► ◄► ◄► ◄► ◄► ◄► ◄► ◄► ◄► ◄►

PURPOSE: To provide practice in the use of dictionary guide words.

GRADE LEVEL: Primary — 3rd grade

TIME: Form A — 25 minutes; Form B — 25 minutes

NUMBER: Best played with a maximum of 16 students

METHOD OF CHECKING: Answer sheet

MATERIALS:
1) 8 sets of 3x4-inch colored posterboard cards bearing dictionary guide words and a word from the page with those guide words. 20 cards to a set, therefore, 160 cards in total are needed. For example:

Guide Words	Words
B/backward	baby
backwards/barely	barber
bargain/basic	bark
be/beaver	beast
became/beetle	bed
billfold/birthday	bingo
bonnet/boot	book
bowling/bran	boy
buff/bulb	bug

The examples were taken from the *Scott, Foresman Beginning Dictionary*.

2) 8 answer sheets dry-mounted to a piece of colored posterboard.

3) Large manila envelope (16x20-inches) for the materials.

PROCEDURE:
FORM A
1) Players pair off with a friend, are given a pack of cards and an answer sheet, and find a place to sit on the floor.

2) The cards are shuffled and placed face down on the floor. The cards may be laid out in any pattern but no two cards should touch each other.

3) The player whose first name is closest to the beginning of the alphabet takes the first turn.

(Procedures continue on page 90)

4) Two cards are turned face up, but left on the floor. If the pair match, the player picks them up, keeps them, and turns up two more cards. The player's turn continues as long as the two cards turned up are a pair. A pair consists of guide words matched with a word that would be found between those guide words.

5) If the two cards are not a pair, they are turned face down and left in their original places and the second player takes a turn. Players may use the answer sheet to check each other.

6) Play continues in this manner until the teacher calls time.

7) The player who has the most correctly matched pairs is the winner.

FORM B

The game is played in the same manner as Form A except the answer sheets are not available for student use.

PURPOSE: To give practice in using guide words.

GRADE LEVEL: Primary — 3rd grade

TIME: 25 minutes

NUMBER: Best played with a maximum of 16 students

METHOD OF CHECKING: Answer sheet

MATERIALS:

1   16 9x12-inch oak-tag Capture gameboards (see illustration on page 92).

2) 8 sets of 4x4-inch colored posterboard cards bearing pictures and names of animals. A free card is to be included in each set. 15 cards per set for a total of 120 cards.

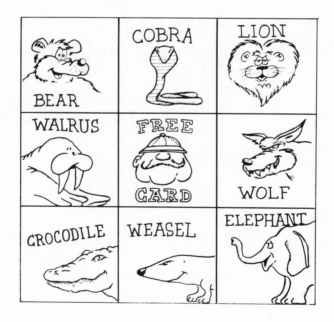

3) 8 answer sheets dry-mounted to a piece of colored posterboard. One example:

(Example follows on page 93)

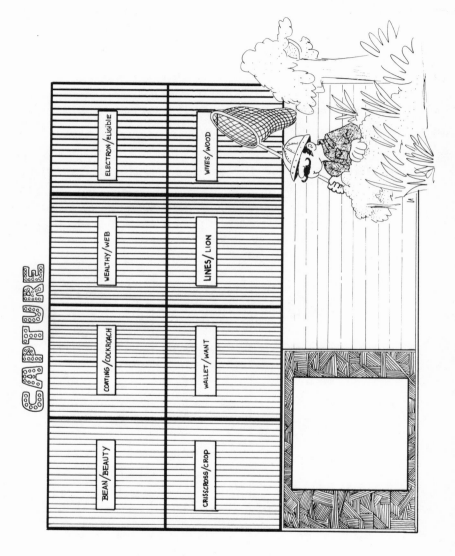

bean/beauty — bear
wives/wood — wolf, wolverine
wealthy/web — weasel
wallet/want — walrus
election/eligible — elephant
coating/cockroach — cockatoo

4) Large manila envelope (16x20-inches) for the materials.

PROCEDURE:

1) Players are paired and each player is given a gameboard. Each pair is given a pack of cards and an answer sheet.

2) The players sit on the floor facing a gameboard. The cards are shuffled and placed in a pile face down between the boards.

3) The players alternately turn up a card until the free card comes up. The player turning up the free card begins the game.

4) The cards are shuffled and placed in a pile face down between the boards.

5) The player turns up a card and attempts to capture the animal by placing it in the correct cage. The correct cage is the one in which the name of the animal falls alphabetically between the two guide words. Players may use the answer sheet to check each other.

6) If correct, the animal is captured and the second player takes a turn.

7) If incorrect, the card is placed back in the pile and the cards are shuffled before play begins.

8) Drawing the free card assures the player of a capture because the card may be placed on any cage and counts as a correct answer.

9) If the player who has used the free card draws the animal that matches the cage covered by the free card, a turn is lost and the animal card is returned to the bottom of the pile.

10) Play continues with players alternating turns.

11) The player who captures the most animals wins.

GUIDE WORD RACE

PURPOSE: To allow students to demonstrate skill in the use of guide words by verbalizing where words are located.

GRADE LEVEL: 3rd and 4th grades

TIME: 25 minutes

NUMBER: Best played with a maximum of 16 students

METHOD OF CHECKING: Teacher

MATERIALS:

1) Chalkboard and chalk, or

2) 4 8x10-inch colored posterboard cards with the words "before," "guide words," and "after" clearly printed on them.

BEFORE	GUIDE WORDS	AFTER
	Take-Tap	

3) 4 sets of 20 3x3-inch colored posterboard cards. The following are suggested guide words and word lists:

Take – Tap		Cage – Camp	
tail	top	careful	cake
tame	tan	can	cabin
tall	tar	calm	cable
tackle	thank	calk	cadet
taught	tabulate	cook	came
talk	tangle	camel	calf
tape	tip	candy	cactus
task	tank	camera	cafe
table	tale	call	cup
tool	time	cape	cast

Find — Fist		Dream — Droop	
fickle	finger	dredge	drench
firm	fix	drink	drip
fit	fill	done	drag
fire	fish	drape	dread
fine	five	drill	dresser
fin	fiddle	drop	drawn
final	few	drew	drift
first	film	dress	danger
fidget	fork	drive	dirt
fox	file	draw	devote

4) Large manila envelope (12x15-inches) for the materials.

PROCEDURE:

1) Divide the students into two evenly matched teams.

2) Either divide the chalkboard into three areas or display one of the 8x10-inch colored posterboard cards.

3) The teacher chooses a number from 1 to 10, in order to determine team order of play.

4) The first student on each team is to guess a number between 1 and 10. The team that guesses the number that matches (or is closest to) the number that the teacher has written down goes first.

5) The cards matching the 8x10-inch card displayed are placed face down on a table.

6) The first player from team one selects a card from the pile.

7) The player must decide in which column to place the word. (If it belongs between the guide words, it is placed in the middle column. If the word does not belong between the guide words, it is placed in either the "before" or "after" column.)

8) When the decision is made, the player either writes the word in the correct column or places the card in the proper category. After it is placed, an explanation as to why it was placed there should be given.

9) If the word is correctly placed, the player scores a point for the team.

10) If it is incorrectly placed, the opposing team scores a point.

11) The first player from team two follows the same procedure.

12) Teams alternate turns until all the words have been used or time is called.

13) The team with the most points at the end of a period wins.

PLURAL PASS

PURPOSE: To provide practice in using the dictionary to locate the plural form of a word.

GRADE LEVEL: Primary—3rd grade

TIME: 25 minutes

NUMBER: The number of available dictionaries or 16 students

METHOD OF CHECKING: Teacher

MATERIALS:
1) Master list dry-mounted to a piece of colored posterboard. The following are a few examples:

   deer—deer or deers
   moose—moose
   mouse—mice
   butterfly—butterflies
   flamingo—flamingos or flamingoes
   canary—canaries
   nursery—nurseries
   goose—geese or gooses

2) One dictionary for each student.

3) Timer.

4) 1 brown paper bag bearing treats or prizes for each member of one team.

5) 2 small chairs and 1 table.

6) Large manila envelope (12x15-inches) for the materials.

PROCEDURE:
1) The students are divided into two teams by counting off in twos.

2) The teacher chooses a captain for each team (this helps to keep order), and all the players line up sitting behind the captains facing the teacher.

3) A small chair is placed facing each captain with a table between the chairs.

4) All players are given a dictionary.

5) The timer is set for 20 minutes and placed on the table facing the two teams. The brown bag is also placed on the table.

6) The teacher calls out a word, and all players use the dictionary to find the plural form of the word.

7) The teacher calls on the first player to raise a hand.

8) The player spells the plural form of the word. If correct, the brown bag is placed on the chair facing that team. If incorrect, the bag stays on the table.

9) If team one has the bag when team two answers correctly, the bag is moved to the chair in front of team two. Each correct answer moves the bag to the chair in front of the team giving that answer. If neither team answers correctly, the bag is returned to the table and the teacher gives the correct answer.

10) This procedure continues until the timer rings.

11) The team who has the bag when the timer rings gets to share the treats or prizes.

◄►◄►◄►◄►◄►◄►◄►◄►◄►◄►◄►◄►◄►◄►◄►◄►◄►◄►◄►
FROM WHAT LANGUAGE???
◄►◄►◄►◄►◄►◄►◄►◄►◄►◄►◄►◄►◄►◄►◄►◄►◄►◄►◄►

PURPOSE: To provide exposure to the fact that the English language has words from other languages.

GRADE LEVEL: Primary—3rd grade

TIME: 25 minutes

NUMBER: The number of available dictionaries or 16 students

METHOD OF CHECKING: Teacher

MATERIALS:
1) Chalkboard, chalk, and eraser.
2) Master list dry-mounted to a piece of colored posterboard. The following are a few examples:

   coma—Greek
   muscle—Latin
   barbecue—Spanish
   clock—Latin
   sky—Norse

3) Class set of dictionaries—the examples for this game are based upon the *Scott, Foresman Beginning Dictionary*.
4) Large manila envelope (12x15-inches) for the materials.

PROCEDURE:
1) Divide the students into two teams by counting off in twos. The teacher chooses captains (to help keep order) and the teams line up behind the captains facing the chalkboard.
2) Give a dictionary to each player.
3) The teacher writes a word from the master list on the chalkboard and all players look up the word in the dictionary.
4) The first player to find the word and from what country it came, raises a hand. The teacher calls on the player to give the answer.
5) If correct, the player scores a point for the team. If incorrect, the opposing team can score a point by giving the correct answer. The teacher calls on the teams alternately until the correct answer is given and a point is scored. If no team answers in one minute, the teacher gives the answer and no point is scored.
6) Play continues in this manner until time runs out.
7) The team who scores the most points wins.

DISCLOSURE

PURPOSE: To provide exposure to the history of words.

GRADE LEVEL: Primary—3rd grade

TIME: 25 minutes

NUMBER: The number of available dictionaries or 16 students

METHOD OF CHECKING: answer sheet or teacher

MATERIALS:

1) Chalkboard, chalk and eraser.

2) Master list dry-mounted to a piece of colored posterboard. The following are examples of words and their histories, taken from the *Macmillan Dictionary for Children*:

   alphabet (p. 21)—comes from the Greek words alpha and beta which are the names of the first two letters in the Greek alphabet.

   America (p. 23)—comes from Amerigo Vespucci, an Italian explorer. It was once believed that he discovered America before Christopher Columbus.

   arena (p. 34)—comes from a Latin word that means "sand." The ancient Romans covered the ground in their arenas with sand.

   astronaut (p. 41)—made up of two Greek words that mean "star" and "sailor." An astronaut is thought of as sailing among the stars.

   bald (p. 50)—the first meaning was "round like a ball." People probably started calling someone without hair bald because a smooth hairless head looks something like a round ball.

   caterpillar (p. 105)—probably comes from an old French word for this insect. The French word meant "hairy cat."

   cheat (p. 111)—long ago it meant "to take back." It was used to describe the way a landlord would take back land if the person who lived there died. Often there were people in the dead person's family who thought they should get the land. They felt that the land had been taken from them unfairly. So the word cheat came to mean "to take something from someone in a dishonest way."

(Materials list continues on page 100)

comet (p. 129)—comes from a Greek word that means "having long hair." The Greeks called a comet a "long-haired star" because a comet's tail looked like long hair flying behind it.

describe (p. 177)—used to mean "to write down." When a person writes something down, he puts it in words. So describe came to mean "to tell about in words," whether the words are written or spoken.

frankfurter (p. 260)—comes from a German word that means "of or from Frankfurt." Frankfurt is a city in Germany, and it is possible that this kind of sausage was first made in Frankfurt.

3) One dictionary for each student.

4) Large manila envelope (10x13-inches) for the materials.

PROCEDURE:

1) Two teams are formed by counting off in twos. The teacher chooses a captain for each team.

2) The teams sit in an orderly line behind the captains, facing the chalkboard.

3) Each player is given a dictionary.

4) The teacher writes a word from the master list on the chalkboard.

5) All players look for the word and raise their hands when they have found it. The player who raises a hand first gives the history of the word as related in the dictionary.

6) If correct, the player scores a point. If incorrect, a point is given to the opposing team and an extra point is scored if that team can give the correct information.

7) Play continues in this manner until time runs out.

8) The team with the most points wins.

PURPOSE: To promote skill in looking up words and discriminating among more than one meaning.

GRADE LEVEL: Primary — 3rd grade

TIME: 25 minutes

NUMBER: The number of available dictionaries or 16 students

METHOD OF CHECKING: Teacher

MATERIALS:
1) Master list of words, their definitions and their illustration numbers dry-mounted to a piece of colored posterboard. The following examples were taken from *Scott, Foresman Beginning Dictionary*.

   agate (1) — a stone with colored stripes or cloudy colors
   boar (2) — a wild pig or hog
   cotton (2) — plant that produces fibers
   dam (1) — wall built to hold back the water of a stream
   elevator (3) — a building for storing grain
   eyeglasses (2) — a pair of glass lenses to help vision
   lasso (1) — long rope with a running noose at the end, used for horses and cattle
   notch (1) — a nick or cut shaped like a V, made in an edge or on a curving surface
   peppermint (1) — an herb grown for its oil, used in medicine and in candy
   seal (1) — a type of sea animal with large flippers, usually living in cold regions

2) Chalkboard, chalk and eraser.

3) Large manila envelope (10x13-inches) for the materials.

PROCEDURE:
1) Two teams are formed by counting off in twos, and each player is given a dictionary.

2) The teacher writes a word from the master list on the board.

3) All players find the word and match the number of the definition to the illustration shown.

4) The player who finds the correct definition first, raises a hand. If correct, a point is scored for the team. If incorrect, the opposing team scores a point and an additional point may be scored if that team can give the correct definition.

(Procedures continue on page 102)

5) Play continues in this manner until all the words are given.

6) The team with the most points wins.

■ ■ ■

◄►◄►◄►◄►◄►◄►◄►◄►◄►◄►◄►◄►◄►◄►◄►◄►◄►◄►◄►
DICTIONARY PUZZLER
◄►◄►◄►◄►◄►◄►◄►◄►◄►◄►◄►◄►◄►◄►◄►◄►◄►◄►◄►

PURPOSE: To give practice in locating categories and words which fit into those categories.

GRADE LEVEL: 3rd grade through 6th grade

TIME: Form A – 30 minutes; Form B – 30 minutes

NUMBER: The number of available dictionaries or 16 students

METHOD OF CHECKING: Teacher

MATERIALS:
1) 1 dictionary for each student.
2) 16 9x12-inch oak-tag "Dictionary Puzzler" cards. For best results, use different categories for each group of four students.

Letters	Sports	Famous Women	Clothing	Famous Men	Fruit	Animals	Birds
B							
L							
C							
M							
S							
T							

(Materials list continues on page 104)

Sample answers:

B—basketball, Mary McLeod Bethune, blouse, Johann Sebastian Bach, banana, badger, blue jay

L—lacrosse, Amy Lowell, leggings, Abraham Lincoln, lemon, lynx, lyrebird

C—cricket, Marie Curie, caftan, John C. Calhoun, cantaloupe, caribou, canary

M—motorcycle racing, Marianne Moore, mitten, James Madison, melon, moose, macaw

S—softball, Jane Seymour, scarf, Jonas Salk, strawberry, sheep, starling

T—tennis, Sara Teasdale, tam-o'-shanter, William H. Taft, tamarind, tiger, thrush

3) 16 Vis-a-Vis® pens.

4) Damp paper towels to wipe off the Vis-a-Vis® markers from "Dictionary Puzzler" cards when game is finished.

5) Large manila envelope (12x15-inches) for the materials.

PROCEDURE:

FORM A

1) Each individual player is given a "Dictionary Puzzler" card, a dictionary and a Vis-a-Vis® pen.

2) The players are to search the dictionary to find the required information beginning with each letter at the left of the columns.

3) When a piece of information is found, the player will write it in the space available.

4) Two points are given for each space correctly filled.

5) The player with the highest number of points is the winner.

FORM B

1) The players are divided into four groups of four.

2) Each group is given a "Dictionary Puzzler" card, a dictionary and a Vis-a-Vis® pen.

3) Each group is to search through the dictionary to find the required information, beginning with each letter at the left of the columns.

4) One player from each group should write the information in the space available.

5) Two points may be given for each space correctly filled.

6) The group with the highest number of points wins.

PURPOSE: To promote skill in looking up information in a dictionary.

GRADE LEVEL: Intermediate—5th and 6th grades

TIME: 25 minutes

NUMBER: The number of available dictionaries or 16 students

METHOD OF CHECKING: Teacher

MATERIALS:
  1) 48 3x4-inch colored posterboard cards (3 for each student) with dictionary questions written on one side.

   Do you caper with your eyes?
   What is a coracle?
   Can you eat a russet?
   Would you use a hamper to play baseball?
   Is a lamprey a lamp?
   Is an aye-aye an animal?
   Would you wear a miter?
   Would you be afraid of an eft?
   Would you pet a lynx?
   Would you like to meet a zebu?
   Do foxes wear fox gloves?
   Is a lemming a lemon?
   Could a car get stuck in gumbo?
   Does brocade mean a cheap cloth?
   Would you wear an abalone?
   Would you be afraid of an aardvark?
   Would you find an abominable snowman in the Rocky Mountains?
   What is the Acropolis?
   Would you like to meet an anaconda?
   Is an appaloosa all one color?
   Would you keep an zxolotl for a pet?
   Does a banyan tree grow bananas?
   Would you bowl a boll weevil?
   Is a boomerang a straight piece of wood?
   Does a breadfruit resemble bread?
   Does a brontosaur make a loveable pet?
   Does a bullroarer roar?
   What is a burnoose?

(Dictionary questions continue on page 106)

Is a cacomistle a cousin to a raccoon?
Is a calumet used as a symbol of war?
Can suspenders hold up suspense?
Is sorghum a new form of gum?
Can a sphinx put a jinx on you?
Would you eat a jacose salad?
Is a carafe the same as a caftan?
Is a cassowary an animal?
Is a guru the same as a gnu?
Can a grackle make a crackle?
Is a gourmand a person who eats like a bird?
Is a horehound a hound?
Is a howdah a ship at sea?
Would a lemur make a good household pet?
Is a hydrofoil a foil?
Is a limpet limpid?
Is a lyrebird a liar?
Is a maelstrom a storm?
What is a megalith?
Is a mime a mine?

2) Class set of dictionaries, one for each student.

3) Large manila envelope (9x12-inches) for the materials.

PROCEDURE:

1) Divide the students into two evenly matched teams, but each student works individually.

2) A dictionary is given to each student.

3) Place half of the question cards face down on a table in front of each team.

4) Each student chooses a card and uses the dictionary to find the answer to the question.

5) When a student has located the answer, a hand is raised to indicate the answer has been found. The teacher checks the answer and the student chooses a second card.

6) When three questions have been answered successfully, a student may help someone else on his/her team.

7) The team that answers all its questions correctly first is the winner.

■ ■ ■

◄►
SCRUTINY
◄►

PURPOSE: To promote skill in the use of the dictionary for locating information.

GRADE LEVEL: Intermediate—4th and 5th grades

TIME: 30 minutes

NUMBER: the number of available dictionaries or 16 students

METHOD OF CHECKING: Teacher

MATERIALS:
1) 1 dictionary for each student.
2) 80 3x4-inch colored posterboard "Scrutiny Cards" with words and questions such as:

   opinion
   How many syllables are in this word?

   new
   How many entries are listed for this word?

   esophagus
   Where is the accent in this word?

   travel
   Is this word found at the beginning, the middle, or the end of the dictionary?

   never
   What part of speech is this word?

3) Master list of words, questions and answers, dry-mounted to a piece of colored posterboard.
4) Large manila envelope (12x15-inches) for the materials.

PROCEDURE:
1) The group is divided into two teams, but each student works individually.
2) Each team member is given a dictionary, chooses a card, looks up the word on the card, and answers the question about the word.
3) The word is shown and the answer is given to the teacher who records a point for that team.
4) As each player answers the question, a new card is chosen.
5) The team scoring the greatest number of points wins.

■ ■ ■

PURPOSE: To give students practice in locating information in dictionaries.

GRADE LEVEL: Intermediate—4th grade

TIME: 25 minutes

NUMBER: The number of available dictionaries or 16 students

METHOD OF CHECKING: Teacher

MATERIALS:

1) 48 3x4-inch colored posterboard cards (3 for each student) with the name of the bird in code on the top one-half and the type of code used on the bottom half of each card.

Bird	Scrambled	Without Vowels	Substituting "z" for Vowels
parrot	rrapot	prrt	pzrrzt
oriole	loorei	rl	zrzzlz
penguin	niugnep	pngn	pzngzzn
wren	newr	wrn	wrzn
falcon	lconfa	flcn	fzlczn
starling	gartlisn	strlng	stzrlzng
owl	lwo	wl	zwl
pelican	nepalic	plcn	pzlzczn
eagle	elgae	gl	zzglz
blackbird	dlbbracki	blckbrd	blzckbzrd
peacock	cockpea	pcck	pzzczck
cardinal	landirac	crdnl	czrdinzl
condor	ondorc	cndr	czndzr
catbird	birdcat	ctbrd	cztbzrd
vulture	tureluv	vltr	vzltzrz
robin	binro	rbn	rzbzn
bluebird	birblude	blbrd	blzzbzrd
thrush	rushth	thrsh	thrzsh
finch	hcnif	fnch	fznch
road runner	oadr unnerr	rd rnnr	rzzd rznnzr
gull	llug	gll	gzll
loon	nool	ln	lzzn
quail	ailuq	ql	qzzzl
grouse	esuorg	grs	grzzsz
canary	naryca	cnry	cznzry
ostrich	richost	strch	zstrzch
bobwhite	hitewbbo	bbwht	bzbwhztz
blue jay	uelb yaj	bl jy	blzz jzy

Bird	Scrambled	Without Vowels	Substituting "z" for Vowels
hummingbird	bdiringmmhu	hmmngbrd	hzmmzngbzrd
killdeer	eerdlilk	lkkdr	kzlldzzr
tufted titmouse	esuomitt tedfut	tftd ttms	tzftzd tztmzzsz
nightingale	alegnightni	nghtngl	nzghtzngzlz
white stork	krost itewh	wht strk	whztz stzrk
puffin	inffpu	pffn	pzffzn
lyrebird	bdrireyl	lyrbrd	lyrzbzrd
dove	evod	dv	dzvz
pheasant	stnaaehp	phsnt	phzzsznt
flamingo	ognilmaf	flmng	flzmzngz

2) Master list of all bird names, codes used, and definitions dry-mounted to a piece of colored posterboard.

3) Dittoed sheet, one for each student, of all the bird names used.

4) 1 dictionary for each student.

5) Pencils and paper for each student.

6) Large manila envelope (12x15-inches) for the materials.

PROCEDURE:

1) Divide the students into two evenly matched teams, but players work as individuals.

2) Place half of the bird code cards face down on a table in front of each team.

3) Each player chooses a card, and breaks the code in order to find the name of the bird.

4) Once the code is broken, the player looks up the name of the bird in the dictionary.

5) When the bird is located, the player either writes the definition on a sheet of paper or shows the teacher the correct definition, and then chooses a second card.

6) When three birds have been unscrambled and their definitions found, a player may help someone else on the team who is having problems.

7) The first team to break the "bird code" and find all the appropriate definitions, wins the game.

8) For each correct bird and definition, a player scores one point.

■ ■ ■

SYNONYM SPRINT

PURPOSE: To promote skill and speed in using a dictionary to find synomyns.

GRADE LEVEL: Intermediate — 5th and 6th grades

TIME: 30 minutes

NUMBER: The number of available dictionaries or 16 students

METHOD OF CHECKING: Self-checking or teacher

MATERIALS:

1) 8 9x12-inch oak-tag "Synonym Sprint" cards:

SYNONYM SPRINT		

2) 80 2x2-inch synonym word cards on colored posterboard; ten per envelope. Words may be chosen from the set of dictionaries available, but the following is a suggested list:

abandon	border	error	kingly	pagan	talisman
advice	calm	fear	last	pale	take
affront	care	fit	laughable	pity	taste
afraid	cause	flock	less	quality	thin
allot	cease	fond	map	ramble	untruth
allow	chart	gaze	mend	raise	upon
animal	chief	ghost	mirth	range	use
anger	contract	gracious	name	refer	vain
apt	desert	haste	need	regret	vein
ascend	devout	have	obtain	reply	whiten
banish	dint	imply	obtuse	rural	whole
base	discuss	include	old	scarce	wide
between	dream	irony	opaque	scorch	wind
bluff	effect	join	order	seem	yet
boast	emblem	keen	pacify	shake	zest

3)   8 6x9-inch envelopes for synonym words cards.

4)   16 Vis-a-Vis® marking pens; eight in each of two colors.

5)   Damp paper towels to wipe off the Synonym Sprint cards when finished.

6)   Class set of dictionaries—one for each student. Words are based upon *Webster's Students Dictionary*.

7)   Large manila envelope (16x20-inches) for the materials.

PROCEDURE:

1)   Divide the students into pairs, and give each pair of students a Synonym Sprint card, 2 Vis-a-Vis® pens, an envelope containing 10 synonym word cards, and a dictionary.

2)   The player on the right (Player A) draws a card and places it in the space that he chooses, looks the word up in the dictionary and writes a synonym on the space with the Vis-a-Vis® pen.

3)   If Player B agrees that the word is a synonym, Player B takes a turn. If not, the teacher is called on to decide if it is correct.

4)   If the synonym is correct, Player A scores 2 points instead of 1, and Player B takes a turn. If it is incorrect, Player B scores the point and takes a turn.

5)   Play continues until one student fills three spaces: vertically, horizontally or diagonally (on the order of tic-tac-toe).

6)   The winner of one pair will be matched against the winner of another pair. The loser will be matched with another loser.

7)   The game may be arranged as a tournament to find the "grand winner."

8)   The envelopes may be arranged to consider individual abilities and numbered 1-8; 1 being the easiest and 8 the hardest.

PURPOSE: To allow students to demonstrate the ability to locate a word correctly in a dictionary.

GRADE LEVEL: Intermediate—5th grade

TIME: Form A—30 minutes; Form B—30 minutes

NUMBER: The availability of dictionaries or 16 students

METHOD OF CHECKING: Teacher

MATERIALS:
    1)   64 3x3-inch colored posterboard "clue" cards.

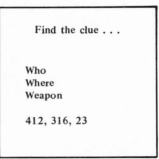

Find the clue . . .

Who
Where
Weapon

412, 316, 23

    2)   Class set of dictionaries—clues for this game are based upon *The American Heritage School Dictionary* (c1972, 1977).

    3)   Pencils and paper.

    4)   Master list of clues and page numbers dry-mounted to a piece of colored posterboard.

    5)   Large manila envelope (12x15-inches) for the materials.

PROCEDURE:
    FORM A
    1)   Give each student a dictionary, pencil, paper and a clue card. The remaining clue cards are placed in an accessible location.

    2)   The object of the game is to discover the answers to these three questions:
       a)   Who did it?
       b)   Where?
       c)   How?

3) The answers are to be found on the dictionary pages marked on the clue card.

4) the dictionary pages will tell who did it, reveal the place where it happened and the weapon used. The pages may have more than one clue; the student will have to decide which one is correct to answer the three questions.

5) When the clues are correctly identified, definitions to the clues are to be written on paper.

6) Form the clues into an imaginative sentence. For example: Beelzebub murdered his victim with amanita in Dar es Salaam.

7) When four clue cards have been completed, the player may help someone who is having trouble.

8) For each clue correctly identified and definition written, the player scores two points. Depending upon the quality of the sentence, from one to three points may be given.

FORM B

To familiarize students with dictionary guide words. The clues could refer only to words and names that appear on the pages as guidewords.

■ ■ ■

PURPOSE: To familiarize students with writing an accurate dictionary definition.

GRADE LEVEL: 3rd grade through 6th grade

TIME: Part I—25 minutes; Part II—25 minutes; Part III—45 minutes

NUMBER: The number of available dictionaries or 16 students

METHOD OF CHECKING: Teacher

MATERIALS:
1) 1 dictionary for each student.
2) Pencils and paper for each student.
3) Crayons, felt tipped pens, pastel chalk, and so on.
4) Drawing paper.
5) 3x5-inch index cards.

PROCEDURE:
PART I
1) Give each player a dictionary.
2) Discuss with the students how to use the dictionaries and how a definition of a person is written: last name, phonetic spelling, first name, birth and death date, and description. For example: CORTES (kôr-tĕz´), HERNANDO. 1485-1547. Spanish explorer, conqueror of Mexico.
3) On the paper, have the students write as many words or phrases as would accurately describe themselves.
4) When this is complete, the students are to rank their words or phrases in order of importance.
5) The players are to use their information to write concise definitions about themselves.
6) The teacher may grade according to creativity and accuracy.

PART II
1) Each student writes his/her description on a 3x5-inch index card.
2) When finished, the students hand the teacher the cards.
3) The cards are shuffled and handed to a student who reads the descriptions to the class.

4) The class tries to guess who fits the description. The "author" does not indicate yes or no until the class has guessed four times.

5) Point value may be given to the writer of the description as follows:

1st try — 4 points (excellent)
2nd try — 3 points (very good)
3rd try — 2 points (good)
4th try — 1 point (fair)

PART III

1) Give each student paper and pencil for sketching a coat of arms.

2) When finished to satisfaction, students are to choose materials and colors to be used for the completed project.

3) Give each student a piece of drawing paper.

4) Demonstrate how to lay everything out on the paper.

5) Students make a preliminary sketch and when finished to their satisfaction, outline and color the appropriate areas.

■ ■ ■

ABC TALK

PURPOSE: To teach students to use a dictionary to assist in creating sentences in which all the words begin with the same letter.

GRADE LEVEL: Intermediate—5th and 6th grades

TIME: 45 minutes

NUMBER: The number of available dictionaries or 16 students

METHOD OF CHECKING: Teacher

MATERIALS:
1) 1 dictionary for each student.

2) Pencils and paper for each student.

3) Master sheet of examples, dry-mounted to a piece of colored posterboard. For example: The triceratops talks to teals.

4) 1 timer.

5) Large manila envelope (10x13-inches) for the materials.

PROCEDURE:
1) Students count off in fours and divide into four or more groups. A team captain is choosen for each group.

2) The team captains pick up one dictionary for each team member.

3) Each team captain is given several pieces of paper and pencils.

4) Each team is to compose as many sentences as it can using the same letter to begin every word in each sentence. For more fun, add a picture.

5) Players are to use the dictionary for added vocabulary and creativity.

6) Set the timer for 20 minutes.

7) At the end of 20 minutes, each team will write its best sentences on a sheet of paper.

8) After the team captains have handed them in, the teacher will read the sentences to the class who will vote on them.

9) Point value could be 1 to 3 points per sentence based on creativity, humor and the following of directions. Students indicate the point value to be given by raising 1 finger, 2 fingers or 3 fingers. Points are tallied by the teacher.

10) When all sentences have been voted upon, the team with the most points is the winner.

11) Optional: Make a classbooklet of all the sentences along with illustrations. Have this as an ongoing project throughout the year as more sentences and illustrations are added.

■ ■ ■

PURPOSE: To show students that pictures can be used to describe objects that are not easy to define.

GRADE LEVEL: Intermediate — 5th and 6th grades

TIME: 25 minutes

NUMBER: The number of available dictionaries or 16 students

METHOD OF CHECKING: Teacher

MATERIALS:
1) 64 3x4-inch colored posterboard cards bearing picture questions like these which are based upon picture captions in *The American Heritage School Dictionary*:

    Where do alligators live? (Only in rivers, lakes and swamps of the Southeast United States and in China.)

    What is another name for aardvark? (Earth pig.)

    How long has the auk been extinct? (Over 100 years.)

    Does a barracuda normally attack human beings? (No.)

    Is the bite of the male species of the black widow spider dangerous? (No, they are small and harmless.)

    For best results, base the picture questions on the dictionaries available for use.

2) 1 dictionary for each student.

3) Master list of all questions and answers dry-mounted to a piece of colored posterboard.

4) Large manilla envelope (12x15-inches) for the materials.

PROCEDURE:
1) Divide the students into two evenly matched teams, but players work as individuals.

2) Give each student a dictionary.

3) Place half of the question cards face down on a table in front of each team.

4) Each player chooses a card with a question that can be answered by looking at the pictures in a dictionary.

5) When the information is located, the player either writes the answer on a sheet of paper or shows the teacher the correct answer, and then chooses a second card. If the answer is written, the student should indicate the page number where the material is found.

6) When four questions and answers have been successfully located, a player may help someone else on the team.

7) The first team to answer all of its questions wins the game.

8) For each answer correctly answered, the player scores one point.

■ ■ ■

WHAT'S IN A DICTIONARY???

PURPOSE: To allow students to demonstrate the ability to locate a word correctly in a dictionary and to recognize and use the correct meaning or definition of the word.

GRADE LEVEL: Intermediate—6th grade

TIME: 45 minutes

NUMBER: The number of available dictionaries and articles or 16 students

METHOD OF CHECKING: Teacher

MATERIALS:
1) Newspaper clippings of articles with words in the headlines that have more than one meaning.

2) Colored paper, glue.

3) Dry mount tissue, laminating film, dry mount press. Clear contact paper will also work.

4) Large manila envelope (16x20-inches) for the materials.

PROCEDURE:
To Prepare
1) Clip newspaper articles with words in the headline that have more than one definition.

2) Underline the word or words (up to 3) to be defined.

3 Choose colored paper for each number of words underlined (e.g., 1-white; 2-red; 3-yellow).

4) Type directions on the colored sheet so that they will appear either alongside or below the article.
   a) One word in the headline is underlined. Your dictionary gives several meanings for this word.
   b) Use the context of the story to determine which definition is the correct one.
   c) Write the correct definition.
   d) Write a sentence that uses the word correctly for the definition chosen.

When two and three words are used, make sure the directions are plural.

To Play

1) Explain to students that this is to be a dictionary game.

2) Read the underlined words from the headlines containing *one* underlined word for a start.

4) Tell students that you have given the words point values based on difficulty (1-3) but it is to remain a mystery to the actual value until they have finished.

5) Do the same for the 2 and 3 word underlined headlines. Students to do one card from each category.

6) Go over the directions with the players. See number 4 under "Procedure: To Prepare."

■ ■ ■

◄►
DO YOU KNOW THE CORRECT DEFINITION???
◄►

PURPOSE: To allow students the opportunity to demonstrate the ability to write a creative sentence and to recognize the correct meaning or definition of a word.

GRADE LEVEL: Intermediate—5th and 6th grades

TIME: 25 minutes

NUMBER: The number of available dictionaries or 16 students

METHOD OF CHECKING: Teacher

MATERIALS:
   1) 1 dictionary for each student.
   2) Chalkboard, chalk, and eraser.
   3) Pencils and paper for each student.
   4) Master list of words and definitions, dry-mounted to a piece of colored posterboard.
   5) Large manila envelope (12x15-inches) for the materials.

PROCEDURE:
   1) Prepare ahead of time a master list of 50 words that are most likely unknown to the students, their definitions, and parts of speech.
   2) Students divide into four or more groups by counting off. A team captain is chosen for each group.
   3) Each team captain picks up one dictionary for each team member, and is given several pieces of paper and pencils.
   4) The teacher picks a word (xenophobe, for instance), writes it on the chalkboard, and gives its part of speech (noun).
   5) Each team must devise its own definition for the word, write it down, and give it to the teacher.
   6) The players then look up the word in the dictionaries.
   7) After all the dictionaries are again closed, the teacher reads the correct definition and the ones supplied by the students. For example:
       A musical instrument that can shatter glass.
       A person unduly fearful of strangers or foreigners.
       A scientific instrument that measures the weather.
   8) Each team must decide the correct definition and tell the teacher its choice. The team who is the first to give the definition to the teacher, gets the first turn to identify the correct definition.
   9) Each team scores points as follows:
       10 points if the team writes down the correct definition.
       5 points if the team chooses the correct definition.
       2 points if the team's definition is chosen as the correct one by the other team.

PART III — ENCIRCLING KNOWLEDGE:
The Encyclopedia and Single Volume Reference Books

What are encyclopedias or single volume reference books? In what section of the IMC/library are they found? Are they difficult to use? Why should we know something about them?

The term "encyclopedia" comes from the Greek word "enkuklios" (meaning "in a circle") and "paideia" (meaning "education"). By combining these two words the Greeks named all knowledge embraced in the "circle of arts and sciences." Today, the volumes bearing this name present past and present facts and theories about man and the universe as accurately as possible. In fact, all the important things that man has ever known or done from the beginning of civilization to the present day can be found in the pages of a good encyclopedia.

There are many kinds of encyclopedias. Some are limited to one subject or to several related subjects. Others give information about all subjects. Some are written for children, others for adults. But they all provide information arranged in such a way that it can be located easily.

Encyclopedias or single volume reference books may be used to answer a fact-finding question, to solve a problem, or to obtain information on a particular topic. They serve as supplements to textbooks, and are not meant to be read through. Once a student learns to check certain parts of an encyclopedia or single volume reference work—the table of contents, index, glossary, copyright date, and text—she or he will understand the purpose of the books and will easily find the needed information. Most are cross-referenced; that is, the reader is directed to a specific place to locate additional information. Related references or materials are also suggested.

However, in order to develop independent study habits, the student should be familiar with the basic types of encyclopedias and single volume reference works. Skill and ease in using them develops only through practice.

The games in this chapter are designed to familiarize students with the many and varied types of encyclopedias and single volume reference books available. However, before using the games in this chapter, it would be wise to review how reference books are organized. The following audiovisual materials would be a good way to spark discussion.

How to Find Information in Reference Books [Sound filmstrip]. Your Library and Media Center: How to Get the Most from Them. White Plains, NY, The Center for Humanities, Inc. 10 minutes, color.

How to Use the Encyclopedia [Sound filmstrip]. Using the Elementary School Library. Chicago, Society for Visual Education, Inc. 14 minutes, color.

How to Use Encyclopedias [Sound filmstrip]. Look It Up: How to Get Information. Mahwah, NJ, Troll Associates. 10 minutes, color.

Getting Acquainted with Sources of Information: Reference Books [Audiocassette]. How to Use the Library (Tape 10). Tulsa, OK, Educational Progress Corporation. 20 minutes.

Getting Acquainted with Sources of Information: The Encyclopedia [Audiocassette]. How to Use the Library (Tape 9, Part I and Tape 10, Part II). Tulsa, OK, Educational Progress Corporation. 20 minutes each tape.

Basic Reference Tools. Using the Library/Instructional Materials Center Effectively. Minneapolis, MN, Creative Visuals, Inc. 11 transparencies, color.

Encyclopedias in the World of Media [Sound filmstrip]. Media: Resources for Discovery. Chicago, Encyclopedia Britannica Educational Corporation. ca.25 minutes, color.

Encyclopedias, Dictionaries and Reference Books. Library Reference Skills. Chicago, Encyclopedia Britannica Educational Corporation. 36 transparencies.

◄► ◄► ◄► ◄► ◄► ◄► ◄► ◄► ◄► ◄► ◄► ◄► ◄► ◄► ◄► ◄► ◄► ◄► ◄► ◄►
DECODE THE MESSAGE
◄► ◄► ◄► ◄► ◄► ◄► ◄► ◄► ◄► ◄► ◄► ◄► ◄► ◄► ◄► ◄► ◄► ◄► ◄► ◄►

PURPOSE: To acquaint students with the alphabetical arrangement of encyclopedias.

GRADE LEVEL: Primary – 3rd grade

TIME: 25 minutes

NUMBER: Determined by the availability of encyclopedias; recommended maximum of 16 students

METHOD OF CHECKING: Teacher

MATERIALS:
1) Various sets of encyclopedias.

2) Book carts or tables on which to place the sets of encyclopedias.

3) Pencils and paper for each student.

4) Master list of encyclopedias (name of set, copyright date) and messages to be used with each set; dry-mounted to a piece of colored posterboard.

5) 48 3x5-inch index cards on which have been written the name of the encyclopedia, the copyright date, and a message in code. Each letter in the message is given the number of the encyclopedia volume that includes that letter. For example: World Book Encyclopedia – 1976. Message: 21/9/1/19 21/1/17 2/14/16/14 18/19/1/14/5/10/14/8 20/15 1/14/5 16/20/14/17 12/21/10/14/8 5/14/21/14? (What was born standing up and runs lying down?) On the back of the card, write the answer in code: 1 12/14/8 3/1/14/14/6. (A log canoe.)

6) Large manila envelope (12x15-inches) for the materials.

PROCEDURE:
1) Before the students arrive, place the encyclopedias to be used on book carts or tables around the room.

2) Students count off in fours and divide into groups of four, one group around a table.

(Procedures continue on page 126)

3) Each player is given paper, a pencil and three message cards.

4) The players are to break the code by placing the numbers, on a separate sheet, then the correct letter beneath the number until the entire message is written out.

5) If a player finishes the three cards before the period is over, he or she may go to one of the library centers for the remainder of the period or continue breaking messages by trading cards with another player who is finished.

6) For each message correctly decoded, the player scores five points.

■ ■ ■

PURPOSE: To provide practice in identifying an encyclopedia volume in which a particular subject is located.

GRADE LEVEL: Primary—3rd and 4th grades

TIME: 25 minutes

NUMBER: Best played with a maximum of 16 students

METHOD OF CHECKING: Self-checking

MATERIALS:
1) 4 (or however many will be needed) 20x14-inch Great Railroad Race gameboards (see illustration on page 128).

2) 4 (or however many will be needed) 20x14-inch drawings of a set of 25 encyclopedia spines. Examples of spines are as follows:

A to Ameri	Horti to Isoto
Amers to Austr	Israe to Lacca
Austs to Blizz	Lace to Madts
Bloch to Calif	Map to Motio
Calig to Chill	Motl to Norwe
China to Conti	Norwi to Peyst
Contr to Dicot	Pfitz to Punic
Dicta to Embry	Punis to Russi
Emera to Finla	Russk to Somer
Finni to Gangr	Sommal to Teleo
Ganna to Greek	Telep to United
Greel to Horth	Uniter to Water
	Watfo to Wymon

3) One marker for each player.

4) 16 (or however many will be needed) letter-size envelopes or cloth pouches.

5) 1 set of 30 3x3-inch colored posterboard cards per gameboard. The front of each card bears an encyclopedia entry; the back bears the volume number in which that entry may be found. 4 sets of 30 cards each set for a total of 120 cards.

(Examples follow on page 129)

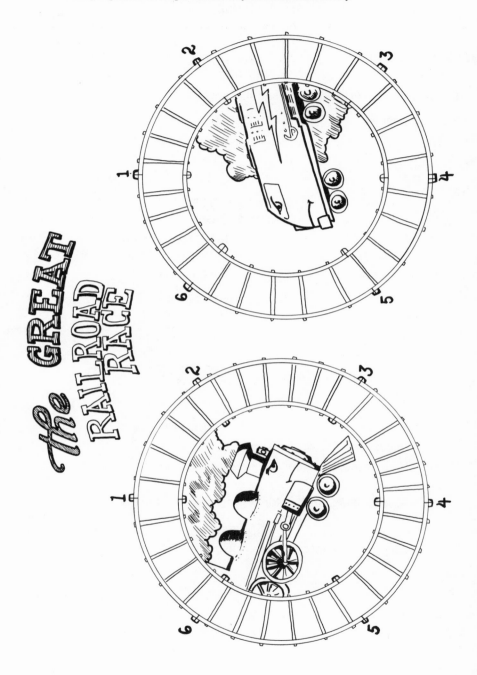

SET I

ACTING
BASEBALL
AUSTRALIA
CACTUS
DINOSAURS
EGG DECORATION
EGYPT
FLYING SAUCERS
FRANCE
GAMES
HANDICRAFT
INDIAN, AMERICA
KNIGHTS AND KNIGHTHOOD
LIONS
MAGIC
CHRISTMAS
BEARS
OUTER SPACE EXPLORATION
RAILROADS
SCIENCE FICTION
TREES
PLANTS
UNDERWATER EXPLORATION
WHALING
YELLOWSTONE NATIONAL PARK
ZOOLOGY
NAVAHO INDIANS
QUAILS
UNITED STATES CONSTITUTION
TEXAS
PAPIER-MACHE

SET II

DICTIONARIES
CHRISTMAS
CALDECOTT MEDAL AWARDS
BOOKBINDING
WITCHCRAFT
SANTA CLAUS
WINTER
HALLOWEEN
OLYMPIC GAMES
SCOTLAND
BASKETBALL
TENNIS
UNITED STATES – HISTORY –
  REVOLUTION, 1775-1783
WOLVES
AFRICA
EARTHQUAKES
HAIKU
OCEANOGRAPHY
PREHISTORIC MAN
UNIVERSE
SASQUATCH
VOLCANOES
BALLET
INSECTS
FLOWERS
GERMANY
BABE RUTH
COLORADO
UNION OF SOVIET SOCIALIST
  REPUBLICS
GREAT BRITAIN

SET III

CANADA, HISTORY OF
CARTOON
CROCODILE
DOGS
BANKS
ALASKA
ADOLF HITLER
FORMOSA
IXTACIHUATL
INTERIOR DECORATION
KING CRAB
JUPITER
KARATE
JELLYFISH
SLAVERY
SABER – TOOTHED CAT
FRUIT
SCOTLAND YARD

SET IV

IRELAND
CRICKET
JAPAN
VIETNAM
WESTWARD MOVEMENT
ZODIAC
YUKON TERRITORY
THOTH
PEARL
GEORGE WASHINGTON
POETRY
MASSACHUSETTS
MODERN DANCE
NORWAY
ABRAHAM LINCOLN
NEW YORK
CHRISTOPHER COLUMBUS
UNITED NATIONS

(Sets III and IV continue on page 130)

SET III (cont'd)	**SET IV** (cont'd)
SUN DANCE	CHINA
ALEXANDER SOLZHENITSYN	POLICE
SPACE TRAVEL	CANCER
TRAP-DOOR SPIDER	MARTIN LUTHER KING
DWIGHT DAVID EISENHOWER	TELEVISION
TASMANIAN WOLF	TACHINA FLY
VOCATIONS	RADIO
JOHN UNITAS	SOUTH DAKOTA
ZUNI INDIANS	STARS
WARSHIP	PLATO
ZEUS	UNION OF SOUTH AFRICA
WAGON	VENUS

6) 1 set of 13 3x3-inch colored posterboard direction cards per gameboard. 4 sets of 13 cards for a total of 52 cards.

   5 cards marked: Return trip — Go back to 1
   4 cards marked: Counterfeit ticket, go back 3 spaces
   4 cards marked: Lucky chance, go ahead 2 spaces

7) Large manila envelope (16x20-inches) for the materials.

PROCEDURE:

1) Players count off in fours and are given a gameboard, cards, and a cloth pouch or envelope.

2) Players are to arrange themselves in alphabetical order by last name, in clockwise fashion, around the playing table. The player with the letter closest to the beginning of the alphabet starts.

3) All players to place markers on start.

4) Cards are shuffled and placed face up on the table near the gameboard.

5) The first player draws a card and names the number of the volume in which the subject of the card would appear.

6) Check the answer on the back of the card.

7) If correct, the player moves the marker to number two. If incorrect, he/she does not move.

8) If a player draws a "return trip" card, he/she must go back to start. All direction cards must be followed.

9) All other players take turns following the same procedure.

10) The first player to go all the way around the track back to start, is the winner.

■ ■ ■

EGG ON

PURPOSE: To promote skill in choosing the correct encyclopedia volume when the volumes are divided between letters.

GRADE LEVEL: Primary—3rd grade

TIME: 25 minutes

NUMBER: Best played with a maximum of 16 students

METHOD OF CHECKING: Answer sheet

MATERIALS:

1) 4 "Egg On" gameboards made out of 14x22-inch colored posterboard.

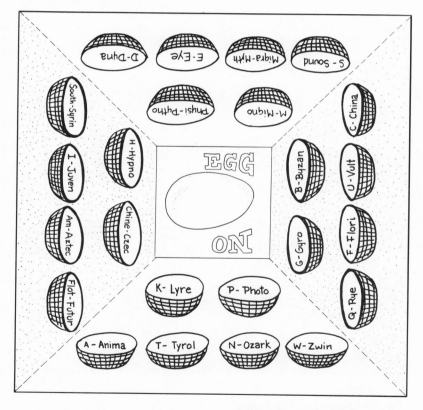

(Materials list continues on page 132)

2) 4 sets of egg-shaped colored posterboard cards approximately 3-inches long bearing topics from the encyclopedia and directions. (Store in a L'eggs® container). 30 cards to a set for a total of 120 cards. Examples of direction cards:

The yolk is on you. Miss a turn.
Sunny side up! Take another turn.
"Eggs-actly" what you need. Free card.
Egg on your face, lose a turn.
Get unscrambled, lose a turn.
No more yolks. Take an extra turn.

3) 4 answer sheets dry-mounted to a piece of colored posterboard. The following example was taken from *Compton's* (1970).

A-Anima	animals
Am-Aztec	anteater
B-Byzan	birds
C-China	chicken
Chine-Czec	chess
D-Dyna	dog
E-Eye	elephant
F-Flori	fish
Flot-Futur	flowers
G-Gyro	giraffe
H-Hypno	hippopotomus
I-Juven	insect
K-Lyre	lion
M-Migno	middle
Migra-Myth	monkey
N-Ozark	North America
P-Photo	panther
Physi-Pytho	python
Q-Rye	rat
S-Sound	snake
South-Syrin	South America
T-Tyrol	tiger
U-Vult	vulture
W-Zwin	zebra

4) 4 dice.

5) Large manila envelope (12x15-inches) for the materials.

PROCEDURE:

1) Players count off in fours and are given a gameboard, cards, die, and answer sheet.

2) Players roll the die to determine the order of play.

3) The cards are shuffled and placed in a pile face down in the center of the gameboard.

4) Player A draws a card, reads it and attempts to place it in the correct basket. Players may use the answer sheet to check each other.

5) If correct, the player keeps the egg shaped card. If incorrect, or the player is unable to use it, the egg is returned to the bottom of the pile.

6) When a card with special directions is drawn, the directions are followed and the card is placed at the bottom of the pile. If a free card is drawn, it may be placed in any basket and counts as a correct answer.

7) The player who fills all the baskets first wins.

■ ■ ■

◄►
WISE UP!!!
◄►

PURPOSE: To provide practice in choosing key words to look up in an encyclopedia.

GRADE LEVEL: Primary—3rd grade

TIME: 25 minutes

NUMBER: Best played with a maximum of 16 students

METHOD OF CHECKING: Teacher

MATERIALS:
1) One flannel board (26x36-inches).
2) A piece of yarn approximately 26-inches long to divide the flannel board in half vertically.
3) 32 3-inch felt owls (an alternative is to duplicate the owls on tagboard, cut out, and glue a piece of felt to each back).
4) A master list of 32 questions dry-mounted to a piece of colored posterboard. Some examples are:
   What is the Milky Way?
   Is the sun a star?
   What does a bear eat?
   How fast can a rabbit run?
   What is a baby goose called?
5) 1 die.
6) Large manila envelope (12x15-inches) for the materials.

PROCEDURE:
1) Two teams are formed by counting off in twos. The teacher chooses a captain for each team.
2) The players line up sitting behind the captain facing the flannel board.
3) The captains roll the die to determine order of play.
4) The teacher calls on the first player to give the key word in the question for finding the answer in the encyclopedia (Milky, sun, bear, rabbit, goose). If correct, the player receives an owl to place on the team's side of the flannel board. If incorrect, the opposing team can get an owl by responding correctly. The opposing team then takes a turn.
5) Play continues with teams alternating turns.
6) The team with the most owls wins.

134

ENCYCLO-SEEK

PURPOSE: To promote skill in locating encyclopedia entries.

GRADE LEVEL: Primary — 3rd grade

TIME: 25 minutes

NUMBER: Determined by the availability of encyclopedias; recommended maximum of 16 students

METHOD OF CHECKING: Teacher

MATERIALS:
1) One or more sets of encyclopedias.

2) 25 3x4-inch colored posterboard cards bearing topics such as:

airplane	eel
bear	fish
clown	giraffe
dinosaur	horse

(Try to duplicate as few letters as possible to avoid waiting for volumes in use.)

3) Large manila envelope (10x13-inches) for the materials.

PROCEDURE:
1) Two teams are formed by counting off in twos, but each student plays as an individual.

2) Each player draws a card (one at a time) from the teacher, chooses the correct encyclopedia, and finds the entry for the topic.

3) The card and the entry in the encyclopedia are shown to the teacher, who scores a point for that team.

4) The player returns the first card, draws another card, and continues playing in this manner scoring as many points for the team as possible.

5) The team with the most points wins.

■ ■ ■

◄►◄►◄►◄►◄►◄►◄►◄►◄►◄►◄►◄►◄►◄►◄►◄►◄►◄►◄►
INDEX PUZZLER
◄►◄►◄►◄►◄►◄►◄►◄►◄►◄►◄►◄►◄►◄►◄►◄►◄►◄►◄►

PURPOSE: To expose students to the index of a reference book, specifically an encyclopedia.

GRADE LEVEL: Intermediate — 4th grade

TIME: 25 minutes

NUMBER: Best played with a maximum of 16 students

METHOD OF CHECKING: Self-checking

MATERIALS:

1) 16 xeroxed pages from the Index volume of an encyclopedia, dry-mounted to a piece of colored posterboard (extra should be included). On the back, draw various irregular shapes in preparation for jigsaw puzzle-type cutting. Give each index page a number, then number each cut-out shape as belonging to one puzzle. Laminate and then cut the pages into various pieces to make the jigsaw puzzle.

2) 16 10x13-inch manila envelopes to keep the puzzle pieces in; each envelope to be marked with the Guide Words and page number. In the lower right-hand corner, place the number for that particular puzzle.

3) Master sheet of questions and answers for each Index Puzzler, dry-mounted to a piece of colored posterboard. Sample questions from page 121 of the Index volume of *World Book Encyclopedia*, 1979 edition, could be:

   Who was Francis Biddle?

   In what volume and on what page will you find a picture of Big Wood River?

   In what volume and on what page will you find information about Big Foot?

   In what state are the Bighorn Mountains located?

   What is Big Boy?

4) Type or letter on 4½x6-inch oak-tag cards or dittoed "problem sheets" like the one below for each index puzzle. Place in the appropriate envelope.

> Looking at the completed puzzle, answer the following questions:
> Who was Whistler, James Abbott McNeill?
> What is a Whip?
> During what period in American history was "When Johnny Comes Marching Home" sung?
> In what volume and on what page will you find information on the Whimbrel?
> What is the Wheatstone bridge?

5) Paper and pencils for each student.

6) An appropriately sized cardboard box or a large manila envelope (16x20-inches) for storing the materials.

PROCEDURE:

1) Give each player a manila envelope, paper and pencil.

2) The players put together the puzzles and answer the questions from the oak-tag card by using the completed puzzle.

3) When finished answering the questions, the player raises a hand to indicate so and the teacher brings the master sheet for checking.

4) One point is scored for each correct answer.

5) When two puzzles have been successfully completed and the questions answered, a player may help someone else who is having trouble.

■ ■ ■

MATH WHIZ WITH INDEXES

PURPOSE: To promote skill in the use of indexes to locate specific information.

GRADE LEVEL: Intermediate — 4th grade

TIME: 25 minutes

NUMBER: Best played with a maximum of 16 students

METHOD OF CHECKING: Self-checking

MATERIALS:
1) Index puzzles used in "Index Puzzler," (page 136).

2) A 6x9-inch oak-tag card with directions, questions, and answers for each index puzzle. Number each card to correspond with a puzzle, then type or letter the information necessary for Math Whiz. For example:

> Notice that the volume is indicated by a letter, then a colon and the page number: "Big Dipper [constellation] B:229 with picture." You are able to quickly learn that the Big Dipper is a constellation — that the article on the Big Dipper appears in volume B on page 229 and that it includes a picture.

> Use this code to determine in which letter volume you will find:
> The location of Big Ben. [B:229, G:328, L:384 and P:153]
> Information about Big Hole National Battlefield. [N:46k]
> John Bidwell's contribution to American settlement. [C:50 and W:210]

> Solve this arithmetic problem using the index page:
> Take the page number on which you will find information about Big Inch. [230]
> Add the page on which you will find a table of the Big Ten. [318]
> Subtract the page on which you will find information on the Big Sioux River. [540]
> Multiply the page number on which you will find the picture of the Big Dipper in the Galaxy. [9] What is your answer? [72]

3) Master sheet of questions and answers for each index page, dry-mounted to a piece of colored posterboard.

4) Paper and pencils for each student.

5) Large manila envelope (16x20-inches) for the materials.

PROCEDURE:

1) Give each player a manila envelope, direction card, pencil and paper.

2) The players put the puzzles together and answer the questions on the oak-tag card by using the completed puzzle.

3) When he or she has finished answering the questions, the player raises a hand to indicate so and the teacher brings the master sheet for checking.

4) One point is scored for each correct answer.

5) When two puzzles have been successfully completed and questions answered, a player may help someone else who is having trouble.

PURPOSE: To familiarize students with the location of specific material in encyclopedias.

GRADE LEVEL: Intermediate—5th and 6th grades

TIME: 50 minutes

NUMBER: Determined by the availability of encyclopedias; recommended maximum of 16 students

METHOD OF CHECKING: Teacher

MATERIALS:

1) 16 (or however many will be needed) 4x8-inch colored posterboard labels with names of famous knights printed in black felt tip pen. For example:

Sir Lancelot	King John
Sir Bertrand	Sir Bors
Sir Galahad	Sir Perceval
King Arthur	Sir Kay
Don Quixote	Sir Tristram
William the Conqueror	Sir Gawain
Charlemagne	Black Knight
Sir Gareth	Sir Geoffroi

2) String or yarn to put through the tops of the "Knight" labels.

3) 16 (or however many will be needed) "Holy Parchment" cards. 3x5-inch colored construction paper.

4) 50 3x5-inch colored index cards on which certain quests have been written. For example:

Your quest is to find an article on "Rauwolfia Serpentina."
Your quest is to find an article on "the Vampire Bat."
Your quest is to find an article on "Greek Art and Architecture."
Your quest is to find an article on "the Kea."
Your quest is to find an article on "Kittiwake."
Your quest is to find an article on "the Teutonic Knights."
Your quest is to find an article on "the Crusades."
Your quest is to find an article on "Fashion."
Your quest is to find an article on "Istanbul."
Your quest is to find an article on "Pioneer Life in America."

5) Various sets of encyclopedias.

6) Large manila envelope (16x20-inches) for the materials.

PROCEDURE:

1) Each student is given a name tag on which is found the name of a knight. The student hangs this around his/her neck.

2) 1 "Holy Parchment" card is given to each student.

3) The students are told that they are knights in shining armour and have many quests to complete.

4) The quest cards are placed face down on a table.

5) Knights are to choose one quest card at a time and find the answer in the various encyclopedias available.

6) When the answer has been found, the knight brings the quest card and encyclopedia to the teacher who checks to see if the answer is correct.

7) If correct, a hole is punched on the "Holy Parchment" card, signifying a correct answer. The quest card is returned to the table and a new one is chosen. If incorrect, the quest is continued until the correct answer is found.

8) At the end of the game, whichever knight has the most holes punched in the "Holy Parchment" is the winner.

■ ■ ■

PURPOSE: To provide practice in locating specific information and in matching it correctly with its counterpart.

GRADE LEVEL: Intermediate—5th grade

TIME: Part I—50 minutes; Part II—50 minutes

NUMBER: Determined by the availability of encyclopedias; recommended maximum of 16 students

METHOD OF CHECKING: Game leader (student)

MATERIALS:
1) Various sets of encyclopedias.
2) 80 3x3-inch colored posterboard cards forming two 40 card sets (based on 16 players). Use 2 different colors—yellow for one set and blue for the other set. On each card, print the name of a baby animal.
3) Dittoed list of adult animals for each student.
4) Pencils and paper for each student.
5) Master list of the adult and baby animals dry-mounted to a piece of colored posterboard.

Adult	Young
cat	kitten
cow	calf
dog	puppy
owl	owlet
fox	cub
hen	chicken
bear	cub
wolf	whelp
dear	fawn, kid
duck	duckling
goat	kid
hare	leveret
lion	cub
swan	cygnet
goose	gosling
horse	colt, filly
moose	calf
sheep	lamb
tiger	cub
eagle	eaglet

Adult (cont'd)	Young (cont'd)
elephant	calf
kangaroo	joey
penguin	chick
giraffe	fawn, calf
camel	calf
impala	lamb
zebra	foal
pig	piglet
whale	calf
rhinoceros	calf
donkey	colt
seal	pup
gazelle	calf
ostrich	chick
llama	kid
hippopotamus	calf
badger	cub
cheetah	cub
bison	calf

6) Large manila envelope (12x15-inches) for the materials.

PROCEDURE:

PART I

1) Each student is given a list of 40 adult animals. Each player must find the name of the baby animal.

2) Students may work in pairs and exchange answers.

3) Students are to study the list in preparation for Part II.

PART II

1) One player is chosen as overall game leader. He/she is given the master list of adult and baby animals.

2) Divide the remaining students into two evenly matched teams. Each team picks a captain.

3) One set of baby animal cards is given to each team captain, who then distributes the cards to team members. Each player should receive at least five cards.

4) The teams line up behind the captains on one side of the room.

5) The game leader is placed at the opposite side of the room.

6) The game leader then calls out the name of an adult animal.

7) One player from each team, who thinks he or she has the correct baby animal card, must *walk* over to the game leader and tag his/her hand.

8) Whichever player tags the hand first receives a point, if the answer is correct.

(Procedures continue on page 144)

9) If correct, the baby animal card is left with the game leader and placed in a pile, either to the leader's left or right depending on placement of team. If incorrect, the player returns with the card to the team to try again. Then, the other team member has a chance to place a card.

10) The teacher is to be beside the game leader in case a dispute over who is right arises.

11) The team that has deposited the most cards with the game leader wins the match.

12) Team captains are to keep track of the points scored by each individual on their teams.

■ ■ ■

PURPOSE: To promote the ability to locate information in encyclopedias and almanacs within a specific time period.

GRADE LEVEL: Intermediate — 5th and 6th grades

TIME: 50 minutes

NUMBER: Determined by the availability of encyclopedias and almanacs; recommended maximum of 16 students

METHOD OF CHECKING: Answer-sheet

MATERIALS:
1) 8 large pairs of bows made from colored posterboard. Paste 12 different colored circles on each; about the size of quarters cut from colored paper. Number the pairs on the back (1-8).

(Materials list continues on page 146)

2) 8 spinners on which are pasted colored circles to correspond with two bows. Indicate set number on back, 1-8.

3) One timer.

4) 8 sets of 24 3x3-inch colored posterboard cards on which are written questions requiring the use of an encyclopedia or almanac. 192 cards in all will be needed. Indicate set number (1-8) on back of each card. In the lower right hand corner place a number 1-24 to correspond with the question on the answer sheet.

5) 8 answer sheets of questions, answers and the reference used — one for every two students. Dry mount to a piece of colored posterboard. For example:

When was the first Superbowl played? Which teams were in it? What was the score? (Almanac) — 1967; Green Bay vs. Kansas City; Green Bay won, 35-10.

Which football team lost the most Superbowl games? (Almanac) — Minnesota Vikings, 4 times.

Are dolphins mammals and are dolphins and porpoises the same? (Encyclopedia) — A dolphin is a small, whalelike mammal whose snout forms a beak. The dolphin is often confused with the porpoise, which has no beak.

What kind of dolphin is most often trained to do tricks in sea aquariums? (Encyclopedia) — The bottle-nosed dolphin because it can be trained to leap high into the air and to grab fish from its keeper's hand.

How do dolphins communicate with each other? (Encyclopedia) — Dolphins communicate by making sounds that include barks, clicks and whistles. Bottle-nosed dolphins even imitate some sounds of human speech.

Why do sailors like to see dolphins when they are at sea? (Encyclopedia) — For hundreds of years, many sailors have regarded dolphins as a sign that their voyage will be smooth and happy.

On what continent is Tierra del Fuego? (Encyclopedia) — South America.

Who was the Grand National Champion in motorcycle racing in 1974? (Almanac) — Mark Brelsford, Los Altos, California.

In what year was Ringo Starr born? (Almanac) — 1940.

How many people were lost in the "Titanic" disaster? (Almanac) — approximately 1,350.

6) 192 plastic tokens or buttons.

7) 8 letter-size envelopes or cloth pouches. Put 24 buttons in each one.

8)   Various sets of encyclopedias and almanacs.

9)   Large manila envelope (16x20-inches) for the materials.

PROCEDURE:

1)   The players are divided into eight groups of 2.

2)   Give each group a set of bows, cards, answer key, spinner and button envelope.

3)   The spinner is placed between the two players, and the cards are placed face down; 12 buttons are counted out for each player and the answer key is placed face down in the center of the table.

4)   The student whose last name is closest to the beginning of the alphabet starts the game.

5)   The timer is set for 2-3 minutes.

6)   The first player draws a card from the face down pile and locates the answer in the encyclopedia or almanac. The player tells his/her opponent the question number and answers the question. The opponent may check the answer key.

7)   If correct, the player gets a chance to spin and win a button for his/her bow. If that color is already covered that turn is forfeited.

8)   If incorrect, the card is placed at the bottom of the pile and the opponent chooses a card.

9)   Stress that a turn must be completed within the time limit set.

10)   The opponent follows the same procedure and the timer is reset.

11)   The player with the most circles covered on his/her bow is the winner.

12)   Each player is to keep track of the number of personal correct answers. For each correct answer, that player scores one point.

■ ■ ■

PURPOSE: To allow students to demonstrate the ability to use an encyclopedia successfully by locating information without constant teacher assistance.

GRADE LEVEL: Intermediate—6th grade

TIME: 45 minutes

NUMBER: Determined by the availability of encyclopedias; recommended maximum of 16 students

METHOD OF CHECKING: Teacher

MATERIALS:
1) Newspaper pictures of sports in action and modes of transportation.

2) Prepared cards with appropriate questions for the sport and mode of transportation. Some sample questions for a picture of a soccer game are:

> Name this sport. (picture of soccer players in action)

> Define "corner kick." (made by an offensive player when a ball last touched by a defensive player passes over the goal line without going into the goal; player kicks the ball from the nearest corner of the field)

> How many players does each team have? (11)

> What is the object of the game? (knock the ball through the opponent's goal)

> When and where was the earliest match played? (400 B.C.; China)

> What does "heading" mean? (hitting the ball with the head)

> There are two ways to kick a ball — using the instep of a foot and the inside of a foot; when are each used? (instep—scoring a goal; inside—passing to a teammate)

> Name the encyclopedia and volume used. (*World Book Encyclopedia* (1976); Vol. 18 (SO-SZ)

> Have you ever participated in this sport?

3) Dry mount the picture on a 6x9-inch oak-tag sheet, above the questions.

4) Pencils and paper.

5) Large manila envelope (12x15-inches) for the materials.

PROCEDURE:

1) Cards are placed in a paper bag or similar mystery receptable.

2) Students must bid for the card; points to be determined ahead of time by the teacher.

3) Make it clear that the questions on the card are to be answered accurately.

4) On signal, students locate the necessary encyclopedia volumes and begin to answer questions.

5) Accuracy and speed both count towards overall team points. One point for each correct answer.

6) Answers are checked by the teacher and reported back to the players.

PURPOSE: To acquaint students with the methods of locating information and answering questions from a single volume reference work.

GRADE LEVEL: Intermediate — 6th grade

TIME: 50 minutes

NUMBER: Determined by the availability of reference works; recommended maximum of 16 students

METHOD OF CHECKING: Teacher/self-checking

MATERIALS:
1) 1 20x14-inch gameboard constructed from colored posterboard for every group of no more than 4 students. Each square should be either yellow or green.

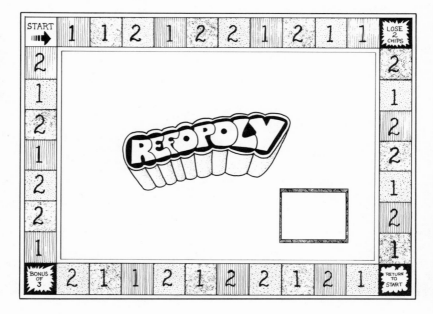

2) 4 dice.
3) 4 sets of 40 3x5-inch colored index cards (20 yellow and 20 green) containing reference questions. In all, 160 cards will be needed. Use each question twice — once on a yellow card and once on a green

card. In the lower right-hand corner, place a number 1-20 to correspond with the question and answer on the answer sheet. The following are some sample questions:

Using *Famous First Facts* who first used 'popcorn'?

In *The Costume Book* what page is Ali Baba on?

Using *Roget's Thesaurus* what is another word for 'glowworm'?

In the *Atlas of the Presidents* which number president was James K. Polk?

Using *The Cowboy Encyclopedia* what is 'larrup'?

Using *In Other Words: A Junior Thesaurus* what is another word for 'lonely'?

Using *Brewer's Dictionary of Phrase and Fable* what is an 'oatin pipe'?

Using *The Trivia Encyclopedia* who was the Red Baron?

Using *Stories of the States* what is the 'state flower' of Hawaii?

Using the *Dictionary of Mythical Places* what is Mirkwood?

4) 30 poker chips per gameboard; 120 in all.

5) 4 markers per gameboard.

6) 4 letter-size envelopes or cloth pouches.

7) 1 bookcart.

8) 1 answer sheet for each gameboard dry-mounted to a piece of colored posterboard. For best results, use a different list for each gameboard.

9) Large manila envelope (16x20-inches) for the materials.

PROCEDURE:

1) 2-4 players arrange themselves in alphabetical order by last name, in clockwise fashion, around the playing table. The player whose last name begins with the letter closest to the beginning of the alphabet starts first.

2) Hand out materials to all groups: gameboard, cards, chips and markers pouch, answer sheet and die.

3) All players place their markers on "start."

4) Player number 1 throws the die and moves his/her marker in the direction of the arrow the number of spaces indicated by the die. If the space landed on is yellow, a yellow card is chosen. If the space landed on is green, a green card is chosen.

5) The player must use the reference source indicated on the card to locate the necessary information. The answer is shown to the group and checked against the answer sheet.

(Procedures continue on page 152)

6) If correct, 1 or 2 chips are given to the player depending on the number indicated on the space, and the card is retained by the player. If incorrect, no chips are given and the card is placed at the bottom of the pile.

7) Play passes on to the next player in a clockwise direction. Or, two players may be looking up information at one time.

8) The player with the most chips is the winner. One point is scored for each chip.

■ ■ ■

THREE GUESSES

PURPOSE: To familiarize students with the various types of reference works and the forms of information that can be found within each.

GRADE LEVEL: Intermediate—6th grade

TIME: Part I—50 minutes; Part II—50 minutes

NUMBER: Best played with a maximum of 16 students

METHOD OF CHECKING: Teacher

MATERIALS:

1) A number of reference works such as:

Our Fifty States
Guinness Book of World Records
Children's Literature Review
Early American Costume
Bartlett's Familiar Quotations
Index to Children's Poetry
Something about the Author
Webster's Biographical Dictionary
Brewer's Dictionary of Phrase and Fable
The New Book of Popular Science
Webster's Geographical Dictionary
Yesterday's Authors of Books for Children
In Other Words: A Junior Thesaurus
Famous First Facts
Junior Book of Authors
Third Book of Junior Authors
Encyclopedia of American History
Stories of the States
The Trivia Encyclopedia
The Cowboy Encyclopedia
Roget's Thesaurus of English Words and Phrases
National Geographic Index, 1947-1976
The Illustrated Encyclopedia of the Animal Kingdom
The Ocean World of Jacques Cousteau

2) Dittoed sheets listing the reference works used; one for each student.

3) 3x4-inch colored posterboard cards with the title of the reference work printed on the front side.

(Materials list continues on page 154)

153

4) A coin of any denomination.

5) Large manila envelope (10x13-inches) for the materials.

PROCEDURE:

PART I

1) Each student is given a copy of the list of titles and should write up three clues for each title to describe the type of information that can be found within each. For example:

1st clue—This reference work is one volume full of essential historical facts.

2nd clue—It is arranged in both chronological and topical order.

3rd clue—Dates, events, achievements and persons of importance are given in narrative form.

OR

1st clue—This reference work contains information on 500 notable Americans chosen for their outstanding achievements in major fields of activity.

2nd clue—Events are arranged in time sequence with annual coverage beginning with the year 1963.

3rd clue—Nonpolitical aspects of American life are examined in detail.

2) Students are to study their sheets in preparation for Part II.

PART II

1) Students are to take the first 5 minutes to look over their papers.

2) Divide the students into two evenly matched teams and choose a leader for each.

3) The team leader whose last name is closest to the beginning of the alphabet is first to call "heads" or "tails" and flips a coin. Whichever team's leader calls the flip correctly is first.

4) Place the cards face down on a table.

5) The teacher starts the game by picking up a card and giving the first clue.

6) The team leader may either answer the question or choose someone on the team to answer.

7) If the reference work is not guessed on the first try, a second clue is given and possibly the third clue.

8) If the answer is correct, the student receives two points and gives the next set of clues. If not, the opposing team has a chance to answer the question correctly and then take its regular turn. In this instance, the teacher should give a new set of clues.

9) The team with the most points wins.

ALLIGATOR ALLEY

PURPOSE: To provide practice in discriminating among the uses of the encyclopedia, the atlas and the almanac.

GRADE LEVEL: Intermediate—4th grade through 6th grade

TIME: 30 minutes

NUMBER: Determined by the availability of materials; recommended maximum of 16 students

METHOD OF CHECKING: Answer sheet

MATERIALS:

1) 4 Alligator Alley gameboards of 20x14-inch colored posterboard (see illustration on page 156).

2) 16 markers.

3) 4 sets of 30 3x4-inch colored posterboard cards bearing questions.

4) 4 master lists of questions and answers dry-mounted to a piece of colored posterboard. For example:

Atlas	Almanac	Encyclopedia
At what latitude is Denver?	What motion picture won the academy award in 1976?	How large can seahorses grow?
Is corn grown in California?	what was the best selling book in 1978?	How fast do radio waves travel?
What is the hottest place in the world?	How many drivers are in Colorado?	Explain how a plane flies.
What place in the world gets the most rainfall?	How much would it cost to fly to London?	Why does the human body need salt?
What is the Northern-most state in the U.S.?	How many branches does the Denver Public Library have?	How many kinds of rhinoceros are there?
What mountain range is east of the Mississippi River?	How many states have nuclear power reactors?	What is heat?
What is the capital of Jamaica?	How many eclipses occurred in 1978?	Can a grasshopper fly?
Compare the vegetation found at 42 degrees North latitude around the world.	What is the average life-span in the U.S.?	How big is a baby giraffe when it is born?

(List continues on page 157)

155

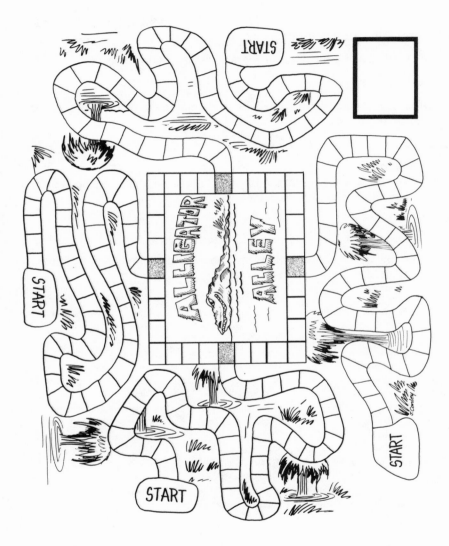

Atlas (cont'd)	**Almanac** (cont'd)	**Encyclopedia** (cont'd)
What is the highest point in the U.S.?	How many deaths occurred in the U.S. in 1976?	When did the first roller coaster appear in the U.S.?
What is the dominant land use in Central America?	How many people in the world speak English?	How long did it take the sculptor to finish Mt. Rushmore?

5) 8 dice.

6) Large manila envelope (16x20-inches) for the materials.

PROCEDURE:

1) Players form groups of four and are given an Alligator Alley gameboard and related materials.

2) Players place markers at start, place cards face down in a pile on the gameboard, and roll the dice to determine the order of play.

3) The first player rolls the dice, draws a card, and answers the question by indicating the correct source. Other players may check the answer sheet for the correct answer.

4) If correct, the player moves the marker the number of spaces indicated by the dice and places the card at the bottom of the pile. If incorrect, the player does not move the marker but the card is still returned to the bottom of the pile.

5) Play continues with players alternating turns.

6) When a player reaches a black space, a choice is made to wait until a double six is thrown on the dice or to travel around the alley toward the start area on the opposite side of the board.

7) The first player to roll double six after reaching his/her own black square or to reach the start area on the opposite side of the board wins.

■ ■ ■

◄► ◄► ◄► ◄► ◄► ◄► ◄► ◄► ◄► ◄► ◄► ◄► ◄► ◄► ◄► ◄► ◄► ◄► ◄► ◄►
REFERENCE BINGO
◄► ◄► ◄► ◄► ◄► ◄► ◄► ◄► ◄► ◄► ◄► ◄► ◄► ◄► ◄► ◄► ◄► ◄► ◄► ◄►

PURPOSE: To review the titles and the types of information to be found within single volume reference books.

GRADE LEVEL: Intermediate—6th grade

TIME: 15-20 minutes each round

NUMBER: Best played with a maximum of 16 students

METHOD OF CHECKING: Teacher

MATERIALS:
1) 16 6x6½-inch colored posterboard Reference Bingo cards with one reference title written in each square (the 25th square is free). the following is a suggested list:

Webster's Geographical Dictionary
Our Fifty States
Book of Marvels
Children's Literature Review
Famous First Facts
A Dictionary of Mythical Places
Early American Costume
National Geographic Index: 1947-1976
Who's Who in Greek and Roman Mythology
The Trivia Encyclopedia
Stories of the States
Brewer's Dictionary of Phrase and Fable
Bartlett's Familiar Quotations
Junior Book of Authors
Third Book of Junior Authors
The Concise Encyclopedia of Sports
Webster's Biographical Dictionary
Roget's Thesaurus
In Other Words: A Junior Thesaurus
Word Origins and Their Romantic Stories
Our Country's National Parks
Index to Children's Poetry
Guinness Book of World Records
The New Book of Popular Science

EARLY AMERICAN COSTUME	ROGET'S THESAURUS	WEBSTER'S GEOGRAPHICAL DICTIONARY	WORD ORIGINS AND THEIR ROMANTIC STORIES	THIRD BOOK OF JUNIOR AUTHORS
CHILDREN'S LITERATURE REVIEW	WEBSTER'S BIOGRAPHICAL DICTIONARY	JUNIOR BOOK OF AUTHORS	NATIONAL GEOGRAPHIC INDEX: 1947-1976	GUINNESS BOOK OF WORLD RECORDS
FAMOUS FIRST FACTS	OUR FIFTY STATES	FREE SPACE	INDEX TO CHILDREN'S POETRY	IN OTHER WORDS: A JUNIOR THESAURUS
BOOK OF MARVELS	BREWER'S DICTIONARY OF PHRASE AND FABLE	THE CONCISE ENCYCLOPEDIA OF SPORTS	BARTLETT'S FAMILIAR QUOTATIONS	STORIES OF THE STATES
THE NEW BOOK OF POPULAR SCIENCE	WHO'S WHO IN GREEK AND ROMAN MYTHOLOGY	OUR COUNTRY'S NATIONAL PARKS	A DICTIONARY OF MYTHICAL PLACES	THE TRIVIA ENCYCLOPEDIA

Each card should be labeled using the titles at random.

2) 320 plastic tokens (20 for each player).

3) 16 letter-size envelopes or cloth pouches for the tokens.

4) One 3x5-inch card for each reference used with the title and a description of the book.

5) Large manila envelope (16x20-inches) for the materials.

PROCEDURE:

1) Each player is given one Reference Bingo card and an envelope or pouch of plastic tokens.

2) The teacher calls off a key description from the index cards and lays the card on the table as a check against the answer the winner calls back at the end of the game.

3) Each player decides which reference work the description fits and places a token on that title.

4) Play continues in this manner until a player covers five correct titles in a row—vertically, horizontally, or diagonally—and calls "Reference Bingo" to indicate he/she has won.

5) When several players call "Reference Bingo" at the same time, each receives a turn at calling out his/her titles, with the teacher checking the index cards.

6) Once a player starts giving the answers, no one else may bingo on that round if he/she did not notify the teacher before the first title is called.

7) If errors occur, explanations are given of why the answer is incorrect and what the incorrect answer refers to, and the game continues.

8) The winning player in each instance is to receive a certain number of points—to be determined by the teacher.

9) Variations of the game:
    a) Four Corners: all four corners must be covered with tokens to win.
    b) Picture Frame: all squares on the outside of the card must be covered with tokens to win.
    c) Black Out: all squares must be covered with a token to win.

■ ■ ■

REFERENCE BOWL

PURPOSE: To allow students to demonstrate knowledge of specific single volume reference works by answering direct questions.

GRADE LEVEL: Intermediate—6th grade

TIME: Part I—50 minutes; Part II—25 minutes; Part III—50 minutes

NUMBER: Best played with a maximum of 16 students

METHOD OF CHECKING: Teacher

MATERIALS:
1) One timer.

2) 16 single volume reference books such as:

   In Other Words: A Junior Thesaurus
   Bartlett's Familiar Quotations
   National Geographic Index, 1947-1976
   Animal Atlas of the World
   Roget's Thesaurus
   Early American Costume
   Guinness Book of World Records
   Junior Book of Authors
   The Every-Day Book
   Famous First Facts
   The Cowboy Encyclopedia
   Encyclopedia of American History
   The Trivia Encyclopedia
   National Geographic Picture Atlas of Our Fifty States
   Atlas of the Presidents
   Webster's Biographical Dictionary

3) One dittoed sheet for each student, listing the 16 single volume reference titles used.

4) Dittoed sheets with blanks for the titles and a concise description of each book used:

   _____: one volume of essential historical facts in both chronological and topical order. Dates, events, achievements, and persons of importance are given in narrative form.

(Materials list continues on page 162)

5) Master list of questions and sources, dry-mounted to a piece of colored posterboard. The following are a few examples:

Who invented Coca-Cola? (*The Trivia Encyclopedia*)
What was the name of the first baseball team? (*Famous First Facts*)
What is the pen name for Margaret Wise Brown? (*Junior Book of Authors*)
What was James Garfield's middle name? (*Atlas of the Presidents*)
What is a 'critter'? (*The Cowboy Encyclopedia*)

6) Master sheet, for the use of the teacher, listing the titles and concise description of the reference books used; dry-mounted to a piece of colored posterboard. For example:

National Geographic Picture Atlas of Our Fifty States — With the map of each state, there is a state story and a quick summary of economic facts. In addition, there are many drawings, photographs and graphs placed in strategic positions.

(For a listing of single volume reference books and descriptions, see Appendix.)

7) Large manila envelope (10x13-inches) for the materials.

PROCEDURE:

PART I

1) Each student is given a copy of the list of 16 titles and is asked to make a good description of each reference work by looking through it. Each student should take notes.

2) Students may work in pairs and exchange the descriptions in preparation for an oral report.

3) After the presentation on each reference work, the class and the teacher ask questions to clarify the description of the reference.

4) Students are to study their sheets in preparation for Part II.

PART II

1) Each student receives a dittoed copy of the concise descriptions of the reference works (number 4 of materials list).

2) Start with an oral drill on the reference works, and have the students fill in the blanks as each title is guessed.

3) For each correct answer, one point is given.

4) Remind students to bring both the list of titles and the sheet of descriptions for Part III.

PART III

1) Divide the students into two evenly matched teams and choose a leader for each.

2) Each team sits in a semi-circle, on the floor or in chairs, with the leader in the middle of the resulting circle.

3) The team leaders are to guess a number between 1 and 10. The number that matches or is closest to the number that the teacher has written down designates which team goes first.

4) The teacher asks any question of the first team and sets the timer for one minute.

5) Team members are to confer with each other to determine in which work the answer could be found, and the leader is to pick someone to answer before the timer rings.

6) If the answer is correct, the team receives two points; if not, the opposing team has a chance to answer correctly and then takes its regular turn.

7) The team with the most points wins.

■ ■ ■

◄►◄►◄►◄►◄►◄►◄►◄►◄►◄►◄►◄►◄►◄►◄►◄►◄►◄►◄►
STUMPER
◄►◄►◄►◄►◄►◄►◄►◄►◄►◄►◄►◄►◄►◄►◄►◄►◄►◄►

PURPOSE: To provide practice in judging where to go for information — the atlas, the almanac, or the encyclopedia.

GRADE LEVEL: Intermediate — 5th and 6th grades

TIME: 30 minutes

NUMBER: Best played with a maximum of 16 students

METHOD OF CHECKING: Teacher

MATERIALS:
1) A stop-watch or a clock with a second hand.
2) Chalkboard, chalk, and eraser.

PROCEDURE:
1) The teacher chooses a player to be the timekeeper and a player to begin.
2) The first player comes to the front and faces the other players who are seated at tables.
3) The timekeeper notes the time on the chalkboard and/or starts the stopwatch.
4) The seated players attempt to stump the player "up front" by asking questions such as:

   What is the population of New York City?
   Who was the winner of the National Chess Tournament in 1977?
   How many kinds of chickens are there in the world?

5) The player does not answer the question, but tells in what reference book the answer could be found. The teacher decides if the answer is correct.
6) If the player can answer all questions correctly, and not be stumped for five minutes, he or she gets to be the timekeeper and chooses another player to come up front.
7) If a question stumps the player, the player asking the question gives the correct answer and comes to the front. The first player returns to his or her seat.
8) Each player scores one point for each correct answer.
9) The player with the most points wins.

PURPOSE: To promote skill in the use of special encyclopedias or single volume reference works.

GRADE LEVEL: Intermediate—5th and 6th grades

TIME: 30 minutes

NUMBER: Determined by the availability of materials; recommended maximum of 18 students

METHOD OF CHECKING: Self-checking

MATERIALS:
1) Book cart with the following reference works or works that include the same type of information:

   Junior Book of Authors
   More Junior Authors
   Third Book of Junior Authors
   Something about the Author
   Yesterday's Authors of Books for Children

2) Paper and pencils for each team.

PROCEDURE:
1) Decide ahead of time which authors are to be used and be sure information is available.

2) Divide the players into teams of six. Each team includes two readers, two messengers, and two scribes.

3) The readers read the article on an author that appears in one of the reference works, and then, without looking at the article, relate the information, with as much detail as possible, to the messengers.

4) The messengers carry the information to the team scribes.

5) The scribes write an article on the author.

6) Compare each team's article with the original article. Are any important facts omitted or any fabrication added?

7) The team with the most accurate article is the winner and scores a number of points determined by the teacher. The other teams score on the basis of their accuracy. *Each team should receive something.*

8) If time permits, players change positions and transmission begins again.

■ ■ ■

PART IV – DISCOVERING THE WORLD:
Atlases, Maps, and Globes

An atlas is a bound collection of maps, charts, tables or plates illustrating any subject. Most historians credit Claudius Ptolemy, a geographer who lived in Egypt, with publishing the first atlas. It appeared in the second century A.D. as part of an eight-volume work on map making. Gerhardus Mercator, a Flemish cartographer, first used the name atlas for a collection of maps published in 1595.

A geographic atlas usually contains charts, maps and tables. Maps can show the topography, soil types and indigenous vegetation. They can show the valuable resources that lie beneath the earth's crust. The daily weather and the climatic conditions of different parts of the world can be shown on maps. Economic and social conditions, population distribution, agricultural production and political boundaries can be charted. The names of such features are usually listed in an index which tells where to find them on the maps. Among the most popular and useful members of the cartographic family are transportation maps which guide us on land, whether we travel by foot, by rail, or in an automobile. But there are also maps for navigating the seas, the air, and even outer space.

Martin Behaim made one of the first terrestrial globes (globes of the earth) in Nuremberg, Germany, in 1492. A globe is a map that has been pasted or printed on a hollow sphere. Only a globe can give a correct picture of the earth as a whole. Because the surface of a globe is rounded like the earth's surface, a globe represents all parts of the earth's surface true to scale. Distances, areas and directions can be observed without the distortion caused by projections used for flat maps. The proportions and positions of land features and oceans, in relation to each other, are seen on a globe exactly as they are on a map.

There is no better way to learn how to read maps and globes than by using them. The language of maps is simple. There are distinctive features and symbols used on maps and globes. Once you become familiar with the "shorthand," you will be able to read and understand them. The following aids can be of help in introducing this unit:

What Is a Map? [Sound filmstrip]. Maps and How to Use Them. Universal City, CA, Universal Education and Visual Arts. 16 minutes, color.

Elements of a Map [Sound filmstrip]. Maps and How to Use Them. Universal City, CA, Universal Education and Visual Arts. 16 minutes, color.

Using Common Maps [Sound filmstrip]. Maps and How to Make Them. Universal City, CA, Universal Education and Visual Arts. 16 minutes, color.

Maps for Special Purposes [Sound filmstrip]. Maps and How to Make Them. Universal City, CA, Universal Education and Visual Arts. 16 minutes, color.

The Globe [Sound filmstrips]. Maps and How to Make Them. Universal City, CA, Universal Education and Visual Arts. 16 minutes, color.

Using the Globe [Sound filmstrip]. Maps and How to Make Them. Universal City, CA, Universal Education and Visual Arts. 16 minutes, color.

Flat Maps of a Round Globe [Sound filmstrip]. Maps and How to Make Them. Universal City, CA, Universal Education and Visual Arts. 16 minutes, color.

Make Your Own Map: Location, Direction and Scale [Sound filmstrip]. How to Read Maps and Globes. Westport, CT, Educational Direction, Inc. 6 minutes, color.

Maps with Special Purposes [Sound filmstrip]. How to Read Maps and Globes. Westport, CT, Educational Direction, Inc. 6 minutes, color.

Getting around the Earth: Parts I & II [Sound filmstrip]. Finding Our Way with Maps and Globes. Burbank, CA, Walt Disney Educational Media Company. 13 minutes each part, color.

The Wonderful Worlds of Maps [Sound filmstrip]. Finding Our Way with Maps and Globes. Burbank, CA, Walt Disney Educational Media Company. 12 minutes, color.

What's on a Map: Parts I & II [Sound filmstrip]. Finding Our Way with Maps and Globes. Burbank, CA, Walt Disney Educational Media Company. 14 minutes each part, color.

Let's Make a Map: Parts I & II [Sound filmstrip]. Finding Our Way with Maps and Globes. Burbank, CA, Walt Disney Educational Media Company. 15 minutes each part, color.

The Message of Maps [Sound filmstrip]. Exploring the World of Maps. Washington, DC, National Geographic Society. 10 minutes, Color.

Using Maps [Sound filmstrip]. Exploring the World of Maps. Washington, DC, National Geographic Society. 14 minutes, color.

The Round Earth on Flat Paper [Sound filmstrip]. Exploring the World of Maps. Washington, DC, National Geographic Society. 12 minutes, color.

The Making of Maps [Sound filmstrip]. Exploring the World of Maps. Washington, DC, National Geographic Society. 15 minutes, color.

Gazetteers and Atlases [Sound filmstrip]. The Library: Our Learning Resource Center. New York, McGraw-Hill. 15 minutes, color.

Map and Globe Skills: Learning Module [Kit and study cards]. Chicago, Society for Visual Education, Inc. 6 sound filmstrips in color; game; continent puzzles; teacher guide; books.

How to Use Atlases and Almanacs [Sound filmstrip]. Look It Up: How to Get Information. Mahwah, NJ, Troll Associates. ca 10 minutes, color.

RUN AROUND

PURPOSE: To provide practice in recognizing directions.

GRADE LEVEL: Primary — 1st and 2nd grades

TIME: 25 minutes

NUMBER: Best played with a maximum of 16 students

METHOD OF CHECKING: Teacher

MATERIALS:
   1)   8 Run Around gameboards made of 9x12-inch colored posterboard.

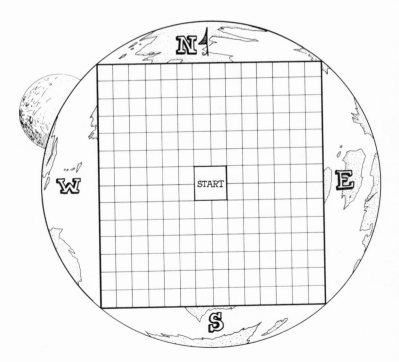

2) 8 packs of 16 3x4-inch colored posterboard cards bearing directions; for a total of 128 cards. Two each of the following make a pack:

1 N	2 N
1 S	2 S
1 E	2 E
1 W	2 W

3) 16 markers.

4) Large manila envelope (12x15-inches) for the materials.

PROCEDURE:

1) Students pair off and each pair receives a Run Around gameboard and related materials.

2) The cards are placed face down in a pile on the gameboard. Players put markers on start.

3) The player whose name begins with the letter closest to the beginning of the alphabet starts by drawing a card and moving the marker the number of spaces and the direction indicated on the card.

4) If there is a question about whether a move is correct, the players raise a hand and ask the teacher.

5) Players alternate turns.

6) A player wins by landing in a space occupied by the opposing player's marker or by going off the board.

HEADING HOME

PURPOSE: To promote skill in the use of directions.

GRADE LEVEL: Primary—1st grade through 3rd grade

TIME: Form A and Form D—15 minutes; Form B—15 minutes; Form C—up to 50 minutes

NUMBER: Best played with a maximum of 16 students

METHOD OF CHECKING: Teacher

MATERIALS:
1) 4 9x12-inch colored posterboard signs bearing: North, South, East, West.

2) 4 small chairs.

3) Masking tape.

4) Chalk.

PROCEDURE:
FORM A
1) Chalk or tape a playing surface 8x8-feet marked off in 12-inch squares.

2) Tape the signs on the chairs and place as illustrated on page 173.

3) Players are divided into two teams and captains are chosen by the teacher.

4) The teams line up behind the captains who stand on either side of the chair marked S, facing the area of play.

5) After the lines are formed, the captain of team 1 moves to the square marked Start 1, and faces the players. The captain of team 2 stands on Start 2 facing the players.

6) The teacher calls on the first player of team 1 to call out a direction. the captain moves 1 square in that direction. If correct, the captain remains. If incorrect, the captain returns to start.

7) Team alternate turns.

8) The first team to place the captain home wins.

FORM B
The game is played the same as in Form A except the chairs with labels are removed.

FORM C

The game is played the same a in Form A except each time a captain reaches home, a point is scored, new captains are chosen, and a new round begins. The team with the most points wins.

FORM D

The game is played the same as in Form A, but on a smaller scale and with more squares using a gameboard like the one below.

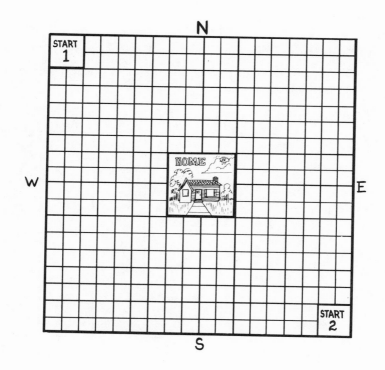

■ ■ ■

PURPOSE: To introduce the use of a grid.

GRADE LEVEL: Primary—1st grade through 3rd grade

TIME: 25 minutes

NUMBER: Best played with a maximum of 16 students

METHOD OF CHECKING: Teacher

MATERIALS:
1) Chalkboard, chalk, and eraser for keeping score.
2) Doober picture on posterboard (22x28-inches) taped to the chalkboard at the students' eye level.

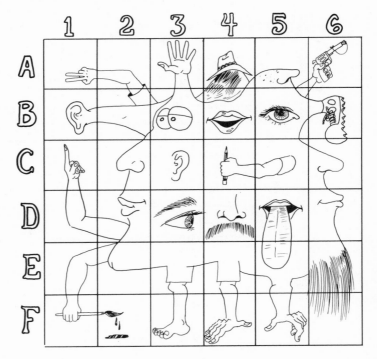

3) A master list of 25 questions dry-mounted to a piece of colored posterboard. Sample questions:

Where is the Doober's ear?
Where is the Doober's upper eye?
Where is the Doober's tennis shoe?
Where is the Doober's tongue?

4) Large manila envelope (10x13-inches) for the materials.

PROCEDURE:

1) Two teams are formed by counting off in twos. Captains are chosen by the teacher.

2) The teams line up seated behind the captains facing the chalkboard.

3) The teacher asks the first player on team 1 a question. The player goes to the picture, points to the part that answers the question, and gives the coordinates (A-2).

4) If correct, the team scores a point and team 2 takes a turn. If incorrect, team 2 can score an extra point by answering correctly. Team 2 then takes its regular turn.

5) Play continues with teams alternating turns.

6) The team with the most points wins.

■ ■ ■

◄►◄►◄►◄►◄►◄►◄►◄►◄►◄►◄►◄►◄►◄►◄►◄►◄►◄►◄►
CAHOOTS
◄►◄►◄►◄►◄►◄►◄►◄►◄►◄►◄►◄►◄►◄►◄►◄►◄►◄►◄►

PURPOSE: To provide practice in using coordinates.

GRADE LEVEL: Primary — 1st and 2nd grades

TIME: 25 minutes

NUMBER: Best played with a maximum of 16 students

METHOD OF CHECKING: Teacher

MATERIALS:
   1) Chalkboard, chalk, and eraser.

   2) 1 die.

PROCEDURE:
   1) Form two teams by counting off in twos.

   2) Two captains are chosen and players line up behind the captains facing the chalkboard.

   3) A grid is drawn on the chalkboard.

   4) The captains roll the die to determine the order of play.

   5) The first player gives coordinates (letter first, then number) aloud and the captain puts an X in that square. If correct, the X remains and team 2 takes a turn. If incorrect, the X is erased and team 2 takes a turn with the captain marking an O.

   6) Play continues with teams alternating turns and captains marking directions given by team members.

   7) A team scores a point when 3 spaces are marked with an X or O horizontally, vertically or diagonally.

   8) After a point is scored the squares of the grid are erased and new captains are chosen.

   9) Play resumes with step 4.

   10) The team with the most points wins.

◄► ◄►
SPLAT
◄► ◄►

PURPOSE: To familiarize students with map symbols.

GRADE LEVEL: Primary—2nd and 3rd grades

TIME: 25 minutes

NUMBER: Best played with a maximum of 16 students

METHOD OF CHECKING: Teacher/self-checking

MATERIALS:
1) 16 fly swatters.
2) 4 sets of 40 3x4-inch colored posterboard "bug" cards bearing map symbols; total of 160 cards. For example:

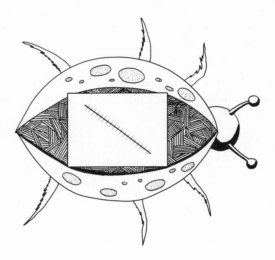

3) Large manila envelope (16x20-inches) for the materials.

PROCEDURE:
1) Players form groups of four by counting off, choose a dealer, and sit in a circle on the floor.
2) The dealer is given a pack of cards and 4 fly swatters.
3) The dealer gives each player a fly swatter and deals out all the cards face down.

(Procedures continue on page 178)

4) The cards are kept face down in a pile in front of each player.

5) The player to the left of the dealer turns up the top card and places it face up next to the face down pile to form a face up pile.

6) Each player does this until any player sees two matching cards face up. The first player to place a fly swatter on one of the two matching cards collects both the pile that card is on and the pile headed by the matching card. The player then places them at the bottom of his or her own face down pile.

7) If two players place fly swatters on the two matching cards at the same time, the matching face-up piles are put together face-up in the center.

8) Players continue to turn over cards and the center pile is won by the first player to place a fly swatter on any players top card that matches the top card of the center pile.

9) When a player has no more face-down cards, the face-up cards are turned back over.

10) Play continues until one player has all the cards.

11) If time does not permit any player to collect all the cards, the player with the most cards wins.

■ ■ ■

PURPOSE: To familiarize students with map symbols.

GRADE LEVEL: Primary—3rd grade

TIME: 25 minutes

NUMBER: Best played with a maximum of 16 students

METHOD OF CHECKING: Self-checking

MATERIALS:
1) 4 sets of map symbol dominoes; a set consists of 28. The dominoes are made of 2x4-inch pieces of colored posterboard. Mimeo the symbols and dry-mount them on the posterboard. A total of 112 dominoes will be needed.

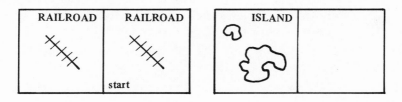

Sample set:

railroad	mountain	island	airport
railroad	mountain	airport	blank
railroad	mountain	island	hill
mountain	island	hill	hill
railroad	mountain	island	hill
island	airport	river	river
railroad	mountain	island	hill
airport	hill	blank	blank
railroad	mountain	airport	river
hill	river	airport	river
railroad	mountain	airport	river
river	blank	hill	blank
railroad	island	airport	blank
blank	island	river	blank

For best results, use different symbols for each set.

2) Large manila envelope (12x15-inches) for the materials.

PROCEDURE:

1) Groups of four are formed by counting off in fours.

2) Each group sits at a table and is given a set of map symbol dominoes.

3) The dominoes are shuffled and placed face down, and each player picks five dominoes.

4) The dominoes that are left are pushed to the side to be drawn later (left-overs).

5) Each player holds the dominoes so the other players can see only the backs of the dominoes.

6) The "start" domino is called and the player holding it begins the game by placing it on the table, face up.

7) The player on the left attempts to match one of the symbols on the "start" domino. If the player does not have a match, dominoes are drawn from the left-over pile until a match is made. Those dominoes drawn are now part of the players hand.

8) If there are no left-overs, the player passes the turn to the player on the left.

9) The first player to play all his or her dominoes wins.

10) If none of the players can make a play and the left-over dominoes are gone, the game ends in a block.

11) All the players count the dominoes held by each individual. The player with the fewest dominoes wins.

■ ■ ■

◄►◄►◄►◄►◄►◄►◄►◄►◄►◄►◄►◄►◄►◄►◄►◄►◄►
SLIP-SLAP
◄►◄►◄►◄►◄►◄►◄►◄►◄►◄►◄►◄►◄►◄►◄►◄►◄►

PURPOSE: To familiarize students with map symbols.

GRADE LEVEL: Primary—3rd grade

TIME: 25 minutes

NUMBER: Best played with a maximum of 16 students

METHOD OF CHECKING: Teacher

MATERIALS:
1) 4 sets of 3x3-inch Slip-Slap cards each made up of 4 cards for each of 13 symbols. A total of 52 cards will be needed for each set.

2) Large manila envelope (10x13-inches) for the materials.

PROCEDURE:
1) Divide the students into groups of four by having them count off in fours.

2) Each group is given a set of Slip-Slap cards.

3) The cards are shuffled and dealt to the students.

4) Each student leaves her/his cards face down.

5) Any left over cards are placed face up in a pile in the center of the group.

6) When play begins, all players turn a card up together and form a second pile of face-up cards in front of them. Note: Students must turn up their cards away from themselves so that all can see the cards simultaneously.

7) When a player sees an identical card turned up to one already on top of any face-up pile, he/she says "Slap" and puts his/her hand flat on the pile.

8) The student receives the two piles topped by the matching cards and places them beneath his/her own face down pile.

9) If anyone slaps by mistake, her/his face-up cards are lost and are placed under the center pile.

10) The student with the most matched cards when time runs out is the winner.

PURPOSE: To familiarize students with map symbols.

GRADE LEVEL: Primary—2nd and 3rd grades

TIME: 25 minutes

NUMBER: Best played with a maximum of 16 students

METHOD OF CHECKING: Self-checking

MATERIALS:
  1) 4 sets of 40 3x4-inch colored posterboard cards bearing map symbols. Each set consists of 2 cards for each of 20 map symbols. A total of 160 cards are needed. For example:

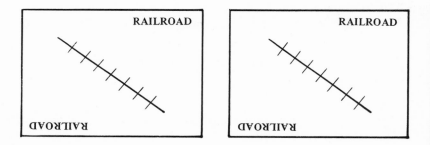

  2) Large manila envelope (12x15-inches) for the materials.

PROCEDURE:
  1) Four to six players gather around a table or in a circle on the floor in alphabetical order.

  2) The student with the last name closest to the beginning of the alphabet is the dealer.

  3) Dealer shuffles cards and places them face down on the table or floor. The cards may be laid out in any pattern, but no two cards should touch each other.

  4) Each player will want to remember the position of each card as it is turned up on the table or floor, since this will help in building pairs.

  5) The dealer starts the game by turning face up any two cards, one at a time. All players look at the two cards as they are turned up, but the two cards are not immediately picked up, just turned face up.

6) If the two cards are a pair, the dealer picks them up, keeps them, and turns up two more cards. The dealer's turn continues as long as the two cards turned up are a pair. A pair consists of two of the same symbol.

7) If the two cards are not a pair, they are turned face down again and left in their original places. This ends the dealer's turn. (Cards are picked up only when they are a pair.)

8) After the dealer's turn is over, the player to the left of the dealer continues the game. Play continues clockwise around the table or circle on the floor.

9) The winner is the player who has accumulated the greatest number of pairs after all of the cards have been picked up from the table or floor.

10) Each player scores one point for each correctly matched pair held by that person at the end of the game.

■ ■ ■

MAP LINGO

PURPOSE: To promote skill in recognizing map symbols.

GRADE LEVEL: Primary—2nd and 3rd grades

TIME: 25 minutes each for Forms A, B, and C

NUMBER: Best played with a maximum of 16 students

METHOD OF CHECKING: Teacher

MATERIALS:

    1)   1 10x12-inch colored posterboard call sheet for the teacher.

    2)   16 different 5x6-inch colored posterboard Map Lingo gameboards.

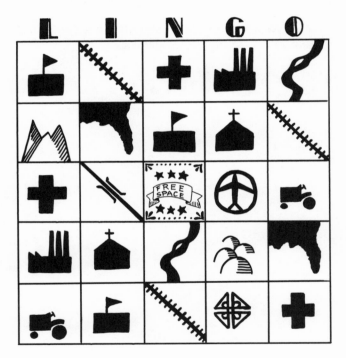

    3)   16 6x9-inch oak-tag sheets identifying all the symbols.

    4)   5x6-inch colored posterboard cards bearing the same symbols as appear on the gameboards. Each symbol card is to be marked with a letter (LINGO) to determine placement in a column. The number will depend upon the number of symbols to be used.

5) 450 plastic tokens, 25 for each player, 50 for the teacher.

6) 17 letter-size envelopes or cloth pouches for the plastic tokens.

7) 1 6x9-inch manila envelope for the symbol cards.

8) Large manila envelope (16x20-inches) for all the materials.

PROCEDURE:

FORM A

1) Each player is given one Map Lingo gameboard, one identification sheet and an envelope or pouch of plastic tokens.

2) The teacher draws a symbol card and holds it up for all to see.

3) A player is called upon to identify the symbol. Players may refer to identification sheets to identify the symbols.

4) The teacher is then to call out the column the symbol is to be placed in, and the correct identification of the symbol.

5) Each player looks at the called column on the Lingo card, and places a marker on the symbol if it is in that column.

6) The teacher places a token in the corresponding space on the call sheet and draws another symbol card.

7) Play continues in this manner until a player covers five correct symbols in a row—vertically, horizontally, or diagonally—and calls "LINGO" to indicate completion.

8) For accuracy's sake, the player should read off the symbols covered so the teacher can check them against the letter and symbol that was called and shown.

9) Variations of the game include:
   a) Four corners—all four corners must be covered with tokens to win.
   b) Picture frame—all squares on the outside of the card must be covered with tokens to win.
   c) Black-out—all squares must be covered with tokens to win.

FORM B

The game is played the same as in Form A except the symbols are not identified orally. Each player must attempt to match the symbol to one on his/her card.

FORM C

The game is played the same as in Form A except that the identification sheets are not used. Symbols are identified from memory.

◄►◄►◄►◄►◄►◄►◄►◄►◄►◄►◄►◄►◄►◄►◄►◄►◄►◄►
JUMP THE BROOK
◄►◄►◄►◄►◄►◄►◄►◄►◄►◄►◄►◄►◄►◄►◄►◄►◄►◄►

PURPOSE: To provide practice in reading a simple map.

GRADE LEVEL: Primary—2nd and 3rd grades

TIME: 25 minutes

NUMBER: Best played with a maximum of 16 students

METHOD OF CHECKING: Teacher

MATERIALS:
1) 16 simple maps of the school on 9x12-inch oak-tag. Include directions on the map.
2) A master list of questions and answers dry-mounted to a piece of colored posterboard. The following are sample questions:

   In what direction is the gym from the IMC?
   Show where you are on the map.
   In what direction do you travel from here to get to your homeroom?
   What are the rooms on the northern end of the school?
   In what direction do you travel from here to get to the principal's office?
3) A 6x1-inch sheet of butcher paper or plastic to simulate a brook. Rocks and ripples may be drawn, colored or painted on the paper.
4) 1 die.
5) Large manila envelope (16x20-inches) for the materials.

PROCEDURE:
1) Each student is given one of the maps.
2) Form two teams by counting off in twos and choose captains.
3) Team members form two lines and sit behind the captains facing the brook.
4) Captains roll the die to determine the starting team.
5) The teacher asks a question of team 1. If correct, the first player jumps over the brook and sits on the other side facing the team. If incorrect, the opposing team has an opportunity to answer the question, have a player jump the brook, and get a second question. If neither team is correct, the teacher gives the answer and teams remain in place.
6) Play continues with teams alternating turns.
7) The first team to jump the brook wins.

186

PURPOSE: To encourage the development of map skills.

GRADE LEVEL: Primary—3rd grade

TIME: 25 minutes

NUMBER: Best played with a maximum of 16 students

METHOD OF CHECKING: Teacher

MATERIALS:
1) 16 road maps of your state (or assorted states).
2) Paper and pencils for each student.
3) Master list of the cities and towns depicting objects, animals, European cities, and so on for the maps used; dry-mounted to a piece of colored posterboard.
4) Large manila envelope (16x20-inches) for the materials.

PROCEDURE:
1) The class is divided into two teams and each student is given a map of a state, a sheet of paper and a pencil.
2) Each student is to list as many towns and cities whose names are also names of objects, animals, European cities, and so on as he/she can within a certain time limit. For example:

Brush, CO	Hamburg, PA	Big Bear Lake, CA
Boulder, CO	York, PA	Elk Hills, CA
Castle Rock, CO	Strasbourg, PA	Los Gatos, CA

3) For every city or town listed within a category one point is given.
4) Points are totaled and the team with the most points wins.

■ ■ ■

◀▶ ◀▶ ◀▶ ◀▶ ◀▶ ◀▶ ◀▶ ◀▶ ◀▶ ◀▶ ◀▶ ◀▶ ◀▶ ◀▶ ◀▶ ◀▶ ◀▶
SOARING
◀▶ ◀▶ ◀▶ ◀▶ ◀▶ ◀▶ ◀▶ ◀▶ ◀▶ ◀▶ ◀▶ ◀▶ ◀▶ ◀▶ ◀▶ ◀▶ ◀▶

PURPOSE: To familiarize the students with the locations of the states.

GRADE LEVEL: Intermediate — 4th and 5th grades

TIME: 30 minutes

NUMBER: Best played with a maximum of 16 students

METHOD OF CHECKING: Self-checking

MATERIALS:
    1)   4 soaring gameboards made from 20x14-inch colored posterboard.

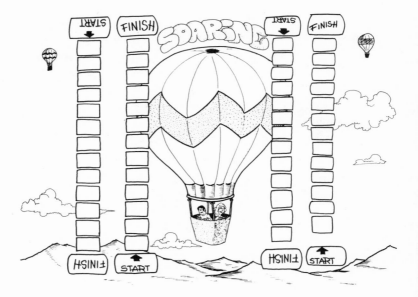

    2)   16 markers (hot air ballons).

3)   4 sets of 3x4-inch colored posterboard cards bearing questions and directions; in all, 128 cards.

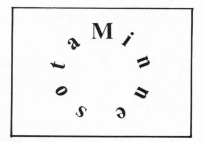

To go from North Dakota to Wisconsin, through what state must one travel?	

Front view   Back view

Sample directions:

Lost ballast, move up one space.
Air is cooling, move down a space.
Hole in the ballon, go back to start.

4)   16 maps of the United States showing state boundaries.

5)   4 dice.

6)   Large manila envelope (16x20-inches) for the materials.

PROCEDURE:

1)   Groups of four are formed by counting off in fours.

2)   Each group gathers around a table and is given a Soaring gameboard and related materials.

3)   The cards are shuffled and placed face down in a pile where designated on the gameboard. All players place markers on start.

4)   The die is rolled to determine the order of play.

5)   The first player draws a card, refers to the map, and answers the question. The answer forms a circle on the reverse side of the card and the player checks to see if his/her answer is correct.

6)   If correct, the player moves the balloon one space upward on the board. If incorrect, the player remains at start. The card is returned to the bottom of the pile.

7)   If a direction card is drawn, the directions are followed and the card is returned to the bottom of the pile.

8)   The player who reaches finish first is the winner.

■ ■ ■

PURPOSE: To provide practice in recognizing state abbreviations.

GRADE LEVEL: Intermediate—4th grade

TIME: 25 minutes

NUMBER: Best played with a maximum of 16 students

METHOD OF CHECKING: Teacher/self-checking

MATERIALS:

    1)   4 sets of 48 3x4-inch colored posterboard cards with states and abbreviations on them. A total of 192 cards will be needed. For example:

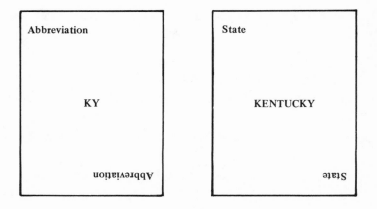

    2)   Master sheet of abbreviations and states dry-mounted to a piece of colored posterboard.

    3)   Large manila envelope (12x15-inches) for the materials.

PROCEDURE:

    1)   Four to six players gather around a table or in a circle on the floor in alphabetical order.

    2)   Student whose last name is closest to the beginning of the alphabet is the dealer.

    3)   Dealer shuffles cards and places them face down on the table or floor. The cards may be laid out in any pattern, but no two cards should touch each other.

4) Each player will want to remember the position of each card as it is turned up on the table or floor, since this will help in building pairs.

5) The dealer starts the game by turning face up any two cards, one at a time. All players look at the two cards as they are turned up, but the two cards are not immediately picked up, just turned face up.

6) If the two cards are a pair, the dealer picks them up, keeps them, and turns up two more cards. The dealer's turn continues as long as each two cards turned up are a pair. A pair consists of a state and its abbreviation.

7) If the two cards are not a pair, they are turned face down again and left in their original places. This ends the dealer's turn. (Cards are picked up only when they are a pair.)

8) After the dealer's turn is over, the player to the left of the dealer continues the game. Play continues around the table or circle on the floor to the left.

9) The winner is the player who has accumulated the greatest number of pairs after all of the cards have been picked up from the table or floor.

10) Each player scores one point for each correctly matched pair held by that person at the end of the game.

■ ■ ■

PURPOSE: To teach students the state capitals.

GRADE LEVEL: Intermediate — 5th and 6th grades

TIME: 30 minutes each for Forms A, B, C, and D

NUMBER: Best played with a maximum of 16 students

METHOD OF CHECKING: Teacher

MATERIALS:
1) 16 State gameboards of 9x12-inch tagboard with states placed in the squares in random order. Each card should be different. Use a different set of gameboards for each group of states — Western, Southern, and so on.

S	T₁	A	T₂	E
COLORADO	IDAHO	UTAH	ARIZONA	CALIFORNIA
UTAH	NEVADA	WYOMING	OREGON	COLORADO
NEW MEXICO	MONTANA	FREE	IDAHO	NEVADA
CALIFORNIA	WASHINGTON	ARIZONA	UTAH	OREGON
MONTANA	WYOMING	NEW MEXICO	COLORADO	WASHINGTON

2) 400 plastic tokens, 25 for each player.
3) 16 letter-size envelopes or cloth pouches for the tokens.

4)   Master list of states and capitals dry-mounted to a piece of colored posterboard to be used as a check sheet by the teacher.

5)   50 2x2-inch colored posterboard cards bearing one of the letters in "state" (S, T_1, A, T_2, E) and a state capital.

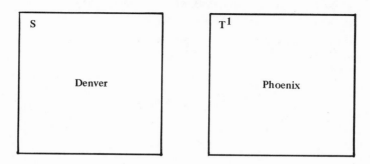

6)   Dittoed list of states and capitals; 1 for each student.

7)   Large manila envelope (16x20-inches) for the materials.

PROCEDURE:
FORM A

1)   Each player is given a State gameboard, an envelope or pouch of tokens, and a list of states and their capitals.

2)   The teacher draws one of the 50 cards and calls out the letter and capital, and marks the answer with a token on the master sheet.

3)   Players may refer to lists to match the capital with the state, and raise their hands when they know the state and capital. The teacher calls on a player for the correct answer.

4)   Players locate the state under the letter called, and place a token to cover the appropriate space.

5)   The first player to cover five spaces horizontally, vertically or diagonally calls out, "State."

6)   The teacher verifies the winning card by checking against the master list.

7)   Players clear cards, trade with a neighbor and play begins again.

8)   Variations of the game include:
   a)   Four Corners — All four corners must be covered with tokens to win.
   b)   Picture Frame — All squares on the outside of the card must be covered with tokens to win.
   c)   Black-out — All squares must be covered with tokens to win.

(Procedures continue on page 194)

FORM B
Played the same as Form A except the correct answers are not given orally.

FORM C
Played the same as Form B without the use of reference sheets.

FORM D
Played the same as Form A except abbreviations are substituted for capitals.

◄►

PICTURE RELAY

◄►

PURPOSE: To promote facility in reading and using coordinates.

GRADE LEVEL: Intermediate—5th and 6th grades

TIME: 40 minutes

NUMBER: Best played with a maximum of 16 players

METHOD OF CHECKING: Self-checking

MATERIALS:

   1)   2 coordinate boards of 14x22-inch colored posterboard.

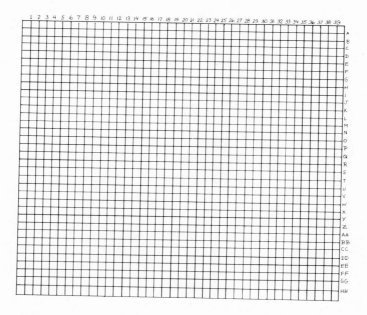

   2)   2 sets of 3x4-inch colored posterboard cards with the coordinates. A total of 96 cards will be needed to complete the picture. Code each set by numbering 1 and 2 on the reverse side. For this picture

(Picture appears on page 196)

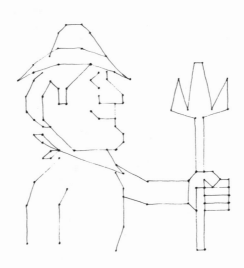

the cards would be labeled with the following directions:

Start		M•22	► N•22	O•13	► O•12	U•35	► U•36
H•10	► F•12	N•22	► O•23	O•12	► P•13	U•36	► Y•36
F•12	► D•15	O•23	► P•23	P•13	► Q•15	Y•36	► Y•33
D•15	► D•18	P•23	► Q•22	Q•15	► R•14	Y•33	► U•33
D•18	► E•21	Q•22	► Q•17	R•14	► R•13	U•33	► V•34
E•21	► H•24	Q•17	► M•13	R•13	► Q•14	V•34	► U•35
H•24	► G•22	M•13	► J•13	Q•14	► Q•15		
G•22	► F•19	J•13	► H•14			V•33	► V•36
F•19	► F•15	H•14	► I•15	R•15	► U•12		
F•15	► G•12	I•15	► K•15	U•12	► X•11	W•33	► W•36
G•12	► H•10	K•15	► K•16	X•11	► CC•11		
		K•16	► I•16			X•33	► X•36
E•14	► B•15	I•16	► F•19	V•16	► X•15		
B•15	► A•16			X•15	► CC•15	Y•33	► DD•33
A•16	► A•18	G•20	► H•19			DD•33	► DD•32
A•18	► B•19	H•19	► I•20	S•22	► U•26	DD•32	► V•32
B•19	► E•21			U•26	► U•31	V•32	► V•33
		N•14	► N•13	U•31	► X•31		
G•21	► H•21	N•13	► M•12	X•31	► X•26	Y•32	► X•31
H•21	► J•23	M•12	► L•11	X•26	► W•23		
J•23	► K•23	L•11	► J•11			T•33	► M•33
K•23	► K•20	J•11	► H•12	T•22	► V•23	M•33	► L•36
K•20	► J•20	H•12	► G•13	V•23	► AA•23	L•36	► H•36
				AA•23	► DD•22	H•36	► L•34
K•22	► M•22	Q•21	► T•23			L•34	► F•33
M•22	► M•20	T•23	► Q•15	U•31	► T•32	F•33	► F•32
M•20	► L•19	Q•15	► O•13	T•32	► T•34	F•32	► L•31
				T•34	► U•35	L•31	► H•30
						H•30	► L•29
						L•29	► M•32
						M•32	► T•32
						Finish	

3)   2 Vis-a-Vis® pens.

4)   Tape.

5)   Damp paper towels.

6)   Large manila envelope (16x20-inches) for the materials.

PROCEDURE:

1)   The coordinate boards are taped to a chalkboard side-by-side at players eye level.

2)   Two teams are formed by counting off in twos.

3)   Captains are chosen and players line up behind the captains facing the coordinate board.

4)   Each captain is given a set of cards and a Vis-a-Vis® pen.

5)   At a signal from the teacher, the first player draws a card, locates the coordinates, and draws a line between them with the Vis-a-Vis® pen, leaves the pen on the chalk rail, and keeps the card. After tagging the next team-member, the player goes to the end of the line.

6)   Players continue in relay fashion until all lines are drawn.

7)   The first team to complete a picture correctly, wins.

■ ■ ■

PURPOSE: To promote skill in using the coordinates of latitude and longitude.

GRADE LEVEL: Intermediate — 4th and 5th grades

TIME: 25 minutes

NUMBER: Best played with a maximum of 16 students

METHOD OF CHECKING: Teacher

MATERIALS:
1) 16 chairs.
2) 2 dice.
3) 2 rolls of narrow crepe paper — 2 different colors.
4) 4 10x4-inch colored posterboard labels to indicate North, South, East, and West.
5) 16 3x3-inch colored posterboard cards with coordinates on them (Example: longitude, 1°W; latitude, 2°N).
6) Large manila envelope (12x15-inches) for the materials.

PROCEDURE:
1) The 16 chairs are arranged in four quadrants to match the coordinates appearing on the cards. The quadrants are formed by one crepe paper line running N—S on the floor and one of the other color running E—W. The four signs (North, South, East, and West) are placed on the floor at the ends of the crepe paper lines:

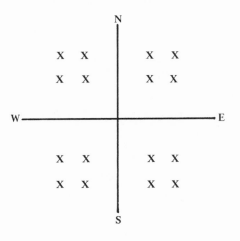

2) Divide the students into two evenly matched teams. Students choose a team captain.

3) 1 die is provided to each team captain who then throws the die for a number. the team with the highest number gets first turn.

4) Each player on team one draws a card and proceeds to hunt for the chair located at the coordinates that are on the card.

5) The teacher checks to see that everyone on the team is at the right place, collects the cards, and scores a point for each player that is correct. Note is made of the players who are incorrect.

6) Each player on team two draws a card and follows the same procedure.

7) The game continues for 15 minutes and the team with the most points is the winner.

8) Players with the correct answer may have free reading or go to centers until end of period.

9) The teacher is to work with those players who were incorrect to explain their errors.

■ ■ ■

PURPOSE: To provide practice in locating latitude and longitude on a grid.

GRADE LEVEL: Intermediate—4th grade through 6th grade

TIME: 30 minutes

NUMBER: From 2 to 16 students, paired

METHOD OF CHECKING: Self-checking

MATERIALS:
   1)   8 dice—1 for each pair of students.
   2)   16 grid cards—1 for each student:

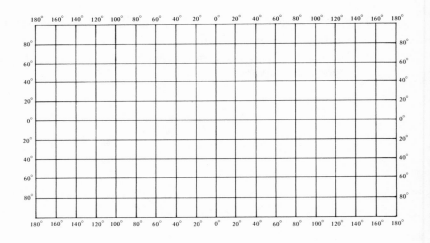

   3)   One Vis-a-Vis® pen for each student.
   4)   Damp paper towels to clean the grid card at the end of the game.
   5)   Large manila envelope (12x15-inches) for the materials.

PROCEDURE:
   1)   Hand out, to each student, a grid card and a Vis-a-Vis® pen.

2) Each player draws 2 submarines on his/her grid card. Each of the submarines should cover 4 squares. they may be placed vertically, horizontally or diagonally. The plotted submarines should not be shown to the other player.

3) Roll a die to see who goes first—highest number goes first.

4) The player who wins the roll of the die calls out a set of coordinates. (Example: latitude 40° north; longitude 20° west).

5) Each player then locates the set of coordinates on his grid card and marks it with an "x" if it is a miss, or a "✓" if it is a hit.

6) If it is a hit, that student takes another turn. Stress honesty about whether the submarine is hit or not.

7) The players continue to take turns until one player sinks both his/her opponent's submarines.

8) For each check mark a point is scored.

■ ■ ■

◄► ◄► ◄► ◄► ◄► ◄► ◄► ◄► ◄► ◄► ◄► ◄► ◄► ◄► ◄► ◄► ◄► ◄► ◄►
SAFARI
◄► ◄► ◄► ◄► ◄► ◄► ◄► ◄► ◄► ◄► ◄► ◄► ◄► ◄► ◄► ◄► ◄► ◄► ◄►

PURPOSE: To allow students to demonstrate the ability to use an atlas, map or globe successfully by locating specific places or information.

GRADE LEVEL: Intermediate — 5th and 6th grades

TIME: 50 minutes

NUMBER: Determined by the availability of atlases, maps and globes or 16 students

METHOD OF CHECKING: Teacher

MATERIALS:
1) Newspaper clippings of names — cities, states, countries; these are best found in the travel section.
2) Two sets of cards (2 different colors) 5x7-inches — 20 per set.
3) Large manila envelope (12x15-inches) for the materials.

PROCEDURE:
1) Dry mount the newspaper names to the cards, then laminate or cover with clear contact paper.
2) Have the students pretend that they are going on a trip to the cities, states, or countries located on their cards.
3) Discuss with the students why it is necessary to find out about the places before visitation — climate factors, part of the world, customs, culture, and so on.
4) Go over or teach how to find latitude and longitude.
5) Review instructions:
   Depending on whether a city, state, or country, give the following information:
   a) city — what state or country is it located in; give the latitude and longitude.
   b) country — what continent is it located on?
   c) state — what part of the country is it located in; give the latitude and longitude for the furthermost extremes of the state.
   d) If an atlas is used — give the page number the information is found on and the map.
6) On signal, the players locate the necessary atlases, maps or globes and begin their Safari in search of the answers.
7) Point value depends on the information correctly answered.

PURPOSE: To show students the locations of countries in relation to their surrounding neighbors.

GRADE LEVEL: Intermediate—6th grade

TIME: 45 minutes

NUMBER: Best played with a maximum of 16 students

METHOD OF CHECKING: Teacher

MATERIALS:

1) 4 packs of 3x4-inch colored posterboard cards bearing drawings of portions of the world. Portions should include only 3 countries each, and there should be 3 cards in each set, as below:

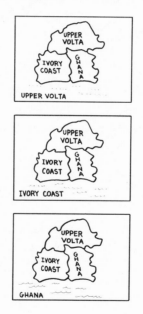

15 sets of 3 cards make a pack, for a total of 45 cards to a pack.

2) Large manila envelope (12x15-inches) for the materials.

PROCEDURE:

1) 3-4 students gather around a table in alphabetical order by the first initial of the last name. If there is more than one student per initial, alphabetize by second letter.

2) The student with the initial closest to the beginning of the alphabet is the dealer.

3) The dealer shuffles the cards and distributes six cards to each player. The remaining cards are placed face down, in a pile, on the table.

4) The dealer begins by asking any of the other players for a card to a set of which he/she holds at least one. For example, if he/she holds the Upper Volta card in the set above, he/she may ask a player, "Do you have the Ghana card?" If that person holds the Ghana card, it must be surrendered.

5) The dealer, having been successful, continues to ask players until he/she asks for a card which a player is unable to give him/her.

6) The dealer then draws a card from those remaining face down on the table, and it is the next player's turn.

7) As soon as one player has all three cards of a set, it is placed on the table in front of him/her.

8) Play proceeds in this manner until all cards are in sets on the table.

9) For each correct set, in front of a player at the end of a game, two points are scored.

■ ■ ■

◄►

PURPOSE: To familiarize students with the locations of countries.

GRADE LEVEL: Intermediate—4th grade through 6th grade

TIME: 30 minutes each for Forms A, B, and C

NUMBER: Best played with a maximum of 16 students

METHOD OF CHECKING: Teacher

MATERIALS:
1) 16 World gameboards of 9x12-inch tagboard with continents placed in the squares in random order. Each card should be different.

W O R L D

NORTH AMERICA	EUROPE	SOUTH AMERICA	ASIA	AFRICA
AFRICA	ANTARCTICA	ASIA	NORTH AMERICA	SOUTH AMERICA
EUROPE	AUSTRALIA	FREE SPACE	AFRICA	NORTH AMERICA
AUSTRALIA	ASIA	NORTH AMERICA	EUROPE	ANTARCTICA
SOUTH AMERICA	NORTH AMERICA	AFRICA	AUSTRALIA	ASIA

2) 400 plastic tokens, 25 for each player.

3) 16 letter-size envelopes or cloth pouches for the tokens.

4) Master list of countries and continents *previously discussed with students*, dry-mounted to a piece of colored posterboard. This is to be used as a check sheet by the teacher. For example:

(Master list is on page 206)

W	O	R	L	D
N.A. Canada U.S. Mexico	**N.A.** Canada U.S. Mexico	**N.A.** Canada U.S. Mexico	**N.A.** Canada U.S. Mexico	**N.A.** Canada U.S. Mexico
S.A. Peru Bolivia Chile Brazil Colombia Argentina	**S.A.** Peru Bolivia Chile Brazil Colombia Argentina	**S.A.** Peru Bolivia Chile Brazil Colombia Argentina	**S.A.** Peru Bolivia Chile Brazil Colombia Argentina	**S.A.** Peru Bolivia Chile Brazil Colombia Argentina

5) 80 2x2-inch colored posterboard cards bearing one of the letters in "world" and the name of a country.

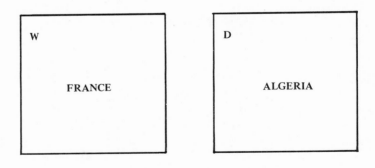

6) 16 small world maps to be used for reference by players.

7) Large manila envelope (16x20-inches) for the materials.

PROCEDURE:
FORM A

1) Each player is given a World gameboard and related materials.

2) The teacher draws one of the 80 cards and calls out the letter and country and marks the answer with a token on the master sheet.

3) Players may refer to maps, and raise their hands when they know the continent matching that country. The teacher calls on a player for the correct answer.

4) Players locate that continent under the letter called, and place a token to cover the appropriate space. The name of the continent can be covered only if it appears in the column under the called letter.

5) The first player to cover five spaces horizontally, vertically or diagonally calls out, "World."

6) The teacher verifies the winning card by checking against the master sheet.

7) Players clear cards, trade with a neighbor and play begins again.

8) Variations of the game include:
    a) Four Corners — all four corners must be covered with tokens to win.
    b) Picture Frame — all squares on the outside of the card must be covered with tokens to win.
    c) Black-Out — all squares must be covered with tokens to win.

FORM B
Played the same as Form A except the correct answer is not given orally.
FORM C
Played the same as Form A without the use of reference maps.

PART V—SPECIAL HONORS:
The Authors

Wide exposure to different kinds of literature and writers brings a delight to most people. They can gain a better self image by reading a book; they have accomplished something. Sad or happy, long or short, stories have moved people through the ages. To be able to create good literature requires genius. Mary Mapes Dodge, editor of *St. Nicholas*, once asked a prospective writer for that magazine "if he was sure he could write something good enough for children." Gifted authors entertain us in joy or sorrow, divert our minds and lead us into delightful places on earth or even through doors that open into other dimensions or universes.

Audiovisual materials that may be helpful in introducing authors are:

Crowell Favorite Authors [20 study prints]. New York, Thomas Y. Crowell. Black and white; biographical notes on the reverse side.

American Literature [Movie]. Chicago, Coronet Instruction Media CORF, 1954. 11 minutes, black and white.

American Tall Tale Heroes [Movie]. Chicago, Coronet Instructional Media CORF, 1974. 15 minutes, color.

McCloskey, Robert [Movie]. Weston, CT, Weston Woods Studio, 1964. 18 minutes, color.

▲▶ ▲▶ ▲▶ ▲▶ ▲▶ ▲▶ ▲▶ ▲▶ ▲▶ ▲▶ ▲▶ ▲▶ ▲▶ ▲▶ ▲▶ ▲▶ ▲▶ ▲▶

CHARACTER OLD MAID

▲▶ ▲▶ ▲▶ ▲▶ ▲▶ ▲▶ ▲▶ ▲▶ ▲▶ ▲▶ ▲▶ ▲▶ ▲▶ ▲▶ ▲▶ ▲▶ ▲▶ ▲▶

PURPOSE: To familiarize students with characters from popular picture books.

GRADE LEVEL: Primary — 1st and 2nd grades

TIME: 25 minutes

NUMBER: Best played with a maximum of 16 students

METHOD OF CHECKING: Teacher

MATERIALS:
1) 4 sets of 3x4-inch colored posterboard cards with reproductions of popular picture book characters on matching cards. There should be one odd character for each set. 51 cards to a set for a total of 204 cards.

2) Large manila envelope (10x13-inches) for the materials.

PROCEDURE:
1) 3-4 students gather around a table in alphabetical order by first initial of last name. If there is more than one student per initial, alphabetize by second letter.

2) The student with the initial closest to the beginning of the alphabet is the dealer.

3) Dealer shuffles the cards and distributes them one at a time until the pack is exhausted.

4) It does not matter if every player does not receive the same number of cards.

5) Players match pairs and place the cards face-down in front of them, without showing them to the other players.

6) All the cards laid out in this manner are left in front of the player, in order to discover errors, if any.

7) The discarding of pairs complete, the dealer begins by spreading the remaining cards, like a fan, and presenting them, face towards herself/himself to her/his left-hand neighbor, who must draw one card at random.

8) The card so drawn is examined, and if it completes a pair, the two cards are discarded.

9) Whether it forms a pair or not, the player's cards are spread and presented to the next player on the left, to be drawn from in the same manner.

10) This process of drawing, forming pairs and discarding is continued until it is found that one player remains with one card.

11) This card is of course the "odd card," and the unfortunate holder of it is the character Old Maid; but only for that deal.

■ ■ ■

PURPOSE: To test comprehension of a story.

GRADE LEVEL: Primary — 1st and 2nd grades

TIME: 25 minutes

NUMBER: Best played with a maximum of 16 students

METHOD OF CHECKING: Teacher

MATERIALS:
1) 1 flannel board (26x36-inches).
2) 2 felt runners approximately 6 inches high.
3) 8 felt hurdles approximately 3 inches high.
4) Master list of 16 questions about one book previously read to the class, dry-mounted to a piece of colored posterboard. Sample questions:

   Why did Petunia think she was wise?
   What did Petunia find in the field?
   How did Petunia help Ida, the hen?
   What did the animals find in the ditch?

   Note: Several lists for different books may be prepared in order to play the game at different times throughout the year.
5) 1 die.
6) Large manila envelope (16x20-inches) for the materials.

PROCEDURE:
1) Two teams are formed by counting off in twos, captains are chosen, and the die is rolled to determine the order of play.
2) Players sit behind the captains facing the flannel board. The felt runners are placed at the left of the flannel board.
3) The teacher reads a question to the first player on team 1. If correct, the team's runner is moved over one hurdle and the player returns to the end of the line. If incorrect, the player returns to the end of the line, and team 2 has an opportunity to move its runner over a hurdle by answering the question correctly. Team 2 then has another turn.
4) If neither team answers correctly, the teacher gives the answer and neither runner is moved.
5) Play continues in this fashion with teams alternating turns.
6) The team moving its runner over all the hurdles first, wins.

■ ■ ■

PURPOSE: To familiarize students with books and their authors.

GRADE LEVEL: Primary—2nd and 3rd grades

TIME: 25 minutes

NUMBER: Best played with a maximum of 16 students

METHOD OF CHECKING: Teacher

MATERIALS:

1) 2 sets of 3x5-inch index cards. Each set should have 50 cards for a total of 100 cards. 25 cards bearing titles and 25 cards bearing authors' names.

2) Master list of authors and titles; dry-mounted to a piece of colored posterboard. A few examples are:

Titles	Authors
The Snowy Day	Ezra Jack Keats
Sam, Bangs and Moonshine	Evaline Ness
Chanticleer and the Fox	Barbara Cooney
Where the Wild Things Are	Maurice Sendak
The Biggest Bear	Lynd Ward
White Snow, Bright Snow	Alvin Tresselt
The Egg Tree	Katherine Milhous
Madeline's Rescue	Ludwig Bemelmans
Song of the Swallows	Leo Politi

3) Large manila envelope (12x15-inches) for the materials.

PROCEDURE:

1) Make sure the students are familiar with the authors and titles used.

2) Divide the students into two evenly matched teams, and choose a leader for each.

3) Give the leader either the title cards or the author cards to distribute to the team.

4) Distribute the other one-half of the set around the room, within reach of the students.

5) Explain that each student must find and bring back to the team leader the matching card so that both cards may be shown to the teacher.

6) Give a signal to start the book hunt.

7) The team with the most correctly matched authors and titles are the winners.

■ ■ ■

PURPOSE: To provide practice in recalling book characters.

GRADE LEVEL: Primary—2nd and 3rd grades

TIME: 20 minutes

NUMBER: Best played with a maximum of 16 students

METHOD OF CHECKING: Answer sheet/teacher

MATERIALS:
1)   4 My Stars! gameboards of 20x14-inch colored posterboard.

2)   4 packs of 32 3x4-inch colored posterboard cards bearing questions.
A total of 128 cards will be needed. Sample questions:

Who drew some adventures with a purple crayon? —Harold
Who was under the haystack fast asleep? —Little Boy Blue
What did Mike call his steam shovel? —Mary Anne
Who dialed the phone, called the fire department, and was put in
      jail? —Curious George

Who gave his mother a bear hug for Mother's Day? — Little Bear
Who was the pet snake that captured a robber? — Crictor

3) 4 answer sheets dry-mounted to a piece of colored posterboard.

4) 4 dice.

5) 16 markers, one for each student playing.

6) Large manila envelope (16x20-inches) for the materials.

PROCEDURE:

1) Groups of four are formed by counting off. Each group is given a My Stars! gameboard and related materials.

2) The players sit on the floor around the gameboard, roll the die to determine the order of play, and place markers on start.

3) The first player shuffles and places the cards, face down in a pile on the designated place on the gameboard, draws a card and answers the question. If correct, the player rolls the die, moves the number of spaces indicated, and places the card at the bottom of the pile. If incorrect, the player remains at start. Players may refer to the answer sheet to check for correct answers.

4) Players continue in this manner alternating turns.

5) The first player to reach finish wins.

PURPOSE: To let students dramatize stories associated with particular characters, learn new vocabulary words, and enjoy group participation.

GRADE LEVEL: Primary—2nd grade

TIME: Depends upon the make-up of the class

NUMBER: Best played with a maximum of 16 students

METHOD OF CHECKING: Teacher

MATERIALS:
1) List of story characters with which the class is familiar. For example:

   Cinderella—stepsisters, prince, stepmother
   Snow White—seven dwarfs, queen
   Rapunzel—husband and wife, witch, prince
   Little Red Riding Hood—wolf, woodsman, grandmother
   Puss in Boots—king, Marquis of Carabas, ogre
   Goldilocks—three bears
   Pinocchio—donkey, toymaker
   The Shoemaker and the Elves—two elves, wife
   Rumpelstiltskin—miller and daughter, king, little man
   Hansel and Gretel—witch, woodcutter, wife
   The Four Musicians—donkey, rooster, dog, cat
   Jack and the Beanstalk—giant, mother
   Three Billy Goats Gruff—troll
   Sleeping Beauty—prince, king and queen, good fairy, evil fairy

2) Art materials—colored paper, crayons, colored pencils, assorted felt-tipped pens, pastel chalk, charcoal, felt squares, scraps of material, and so on.

PROCEDURE:
1) Assign names of characters to students.

2) To avoid confusion later, write down each student's name beside the name of the story character assigned to him or her.

3) At the completion of character assignment, the teacher says, "When I call the title of a story, all students with a part in that story must find their partners."

4) The students are to form groups until all titles have been named.

5) Students should familiarize themselves with the story and characters, and prepare their own story or play.
6) Make art materials available for drawings or costumes.
7) The end product of each group should be shared with the entire group.

■ ■ ■

▲▶ ▲▶ ▲▶ ▲▶ ▲▶ ▲▶ ▲▶ ▲▶ ▲▶ ▲▶ ▲▶ ▲▶ ▲▶ ▲▶ ▲▶ ▲▶ ▲▶ ▲▶
HONEY BEE
▲▶ ▲▶ ▲▶ ▲▶ ▲▶ ▲▶ ▲▶ ▲▶ ▲▶ ▲▶ ▲▶ ▲▶ ▲▶ ▲▶ ▲▶ ▲▶ ▲▶ ▲▶

PURPOSE: To let students display their familiarity with words spoken by book characters.

GRADE LEVEL: Primary—2nd and 3rd grades

TIME: 25 minutes

NUMBER: Best played with a maximum of 16 students

METHOD OF CHECKING: Answer sheet/teacher

MATERIALS:
1) 4 Honey Bee gameboards constructed from 20x14-inch colored posterboard.

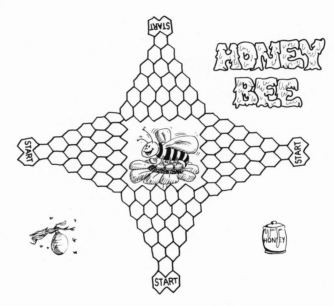

2) 4 packs of 32 3x4-inch colored posterboard cards bearing questions. A total of 128 cards will be needed. sample questions:

Who said, "Mirror, mirror on the wall, who is the fairest of them all?" [Wicked Queen in *Snow White*]

Who said, "Who's that tramping over my bridge?" [Troll]

Who called the public library Mike's house? [Robert]

Who said, "Not by the hair on my chinny chin chin"? [Pig]

Who said, "One-two I hate the zoo.
    Three-four I go to the store.
    Five-six I hunt for trick"? [Little Bear]

3) 4 answer sheets dry-mounted to a piece of colored posterboard.

4) 4 dice.

5) 16 markers (bees or bee shaped, if possible).

6) 4 letter-sized envelopes or cloth pouches.

7) Large manila envelope (16x20-inches) for the materials.

PROCEDURE:

1) Groups of four are formed by counting off. Note: teacher may want to arrange players in order to have at least one good reader in the group.

2) Each group is given a Honey Bee gameboard and related materials.

3) The players sit on the floor around the gameboard, place markers on start and roll the die to determine the order of play.

4) The first player shuffles and places the cards face-down in a pile on the gameboard, draws a card and answers the question. If correct, the player rolls the die and moves the number of spaces indicated, and places the card at the bottom of the pile. If incorrect, the player remains at start. Players may refer to the answer sheet to check for correct answers.

5) Players continue in this manner alternating turns.

6) The first player to cross the board and reach the opposite start wins.

■ ■ ■

◄► ◄► ◄► ◄► ◄► ◄► ◄► ◄► ◄► ◄► ◄► ◄► ◄► ◄► ◄► ◄► ◄► ◄► ◄►
BOOK COVER PUZZLES
◄► ◄► ◄► ◄► ◄► ◄► ◄► ◄► ◄► ◄► ◄► ◄► ◄► ◄► ◄► ◄► ◄► ◄► ◄►

PURPOSE: To familiarize students with the Caldecott books and others, and to foster cooperation among the participants.

GRADE LEVEL: Primary — 3rd grade

TIME: 30 minutes

NUMBER: Best played with a maximum of 16 students

METHOD OF CHECKING: Self-checking

MATERIALS:
1) 32 Caldecott winner or other author book jackets mounted on heavy cardboard or colored posterboard. (On the back, draw various irregular shapes in preparation for jigsaw puzzle-type cutting. Give each set of four puzzles a number, then number each cut-out shape as belonging to one set.) Laminate and then cut the jackets into various pieces to make the jigsaw puzzle.
2) 8 10x13-inch manila envelopes to keep the puzzle pieces in. In the lower right-hand corner, place the number for that particular set (1-8).
3) An appropriately sized box to store the materials.

PROCEDURE:
1) Players count off in fours, and are given a manila envelope of puzzle pieces.
2) Players are to arrange themselves in alphabetical order by last name, in clockwise fashion, around the playing table. The player whose name begins with the letter closest to the beginning of the alphabet starts.
3) The first player becomes the dealer and distributes the puzzle pieces one at a time until all are exhausted.
4) It does not matter if every player does not receive the same number of pieces.
5) The dealer begins and points to a piece he/she wants from another player. The other player must give up that piece and receives a piece the dealer does not want.
6) Throughout the game there should be absolutely no talking; pointing only.

7) The players continue taking turns until all have completed a puzzle.

8) Each player to finish a puzzle correctly scores 5-10 points.

9) Option: The second time around, pieces are placed face-down to make it harder. When pieces fit together, turn them over and continue working.

CALDECOTT BUZZ

PURPOSE: To acquaint students with Caldecott books and with the types of stories to be found within each one.

GRADE LEVEL: Primary—3rd Grade

TIME: Part I—30 minutes; Part II—50 minutes

NUMBER: Best played with a maximum of 16 students

METHOD OF CHECKING: Teacher

MATERIALS:
1) Caldecott books—one for each student participating.
2) Paper and pencils—enough for each student.
3) Ditto masters.

PROCEDURE:

PART I
1) Pass out a Caldecott book to each player who should read the book thoroughly.
2) Players are not to tell each other which book they are reading.
3) On the sheet of paper, write down: a) author and title, b) the main characters and two sentences describing or telling about the characters, and c) a paragraph telling about the story.
4) If the players do not finish within one period time limit, they are to take the book home and finish the assignment, bringing it back before the next meeting.
5) When all sheets have been returned, the teacher should type up each player's paper on a master and run it off; a copy of each for each student. Do not indicate which player has read which book. For example:

> *Arrow to the Sun* by Gerald McDermott
> Characters:
>> Boy—a Pueblo lad who goes in search of his father and eventually finds him in the form of the sun.
>>
>> Corn planter—a person who boy asks to direct him to his father, he does not answer but continues to tend his crops.
>>
>> Pot maker—the second person to be asked but she continues to make her clay pots.
>>
>> Arrow maker—a wise old man who creates a special arrow in the form of boy, and thus boy traveled to the sun.
>>
>> Lord of the Sun—sets trials for boy before he acknowledges him as his son.

"Long ago the Lord of the Sun sent the spark of life to earth, where it entered the dwelling of a young maiden. In this way the Boy came into the world of men. And when the other boys mocked him because he had no father, the boy set out on the Trail of Life to search for him."

PART II

1) Players are to arrange themselves in a circle on the floor with the teacher as a part of the circle.

2) The teacher starts by saying the number 1, and the count continues clockwise around the circle. The student whose number is 5 (or 7, depending on how far players are with the multiplication tables) must substitute the word, Buzz, for the number.

3) The player who substitutes Buzz for the number must then give a sentence describing his/her book or a character in it, but not the title.

4) Play continues in this manner with students "buzzing" on multiples of 5 (or 7) until each player has had a chance to tell about his/her book.

5) The teacher hands out the dittoed sheets and players are to read through them, studying each section to become familiar with the titles, characters and stories.

6) This time around the circle the first player to say Buzz must give a mysterious clue to his/her book and the second player to say Buzz must give the title of the book.

7) If the title is correct, he scores a point and gives a clue to his/her book. If incorrect, play passes on to the next Buzz player who tries to give the correct information.

8) Players may use the dittoed sheets or rely on memory to guess the title.

9) Play continues in this manner until all players have a turn to give clues and to guess titles.

10) If time remains, discuss the books read in detail.

■ ■ ■

◄► ◄► ◄► ◄► ◄► ◄► ◄► ◄► ◄► ◄► ◄► ◄► ◄► ◄► ◄► ◄► ◄► ◄► ◄►
AUTHOR-TITLE ASSOCIATIONS
◄► ◄► ◄► ◄► ◄► ◄► ◄► ◄► ◄► ◄► ◄► ◄► ◄► ◄► ◄► ◄► ◄► ◄► ◄►

PURPOSE: To familiarize students with the Caldecott books, to collect appropriate pictures, and to verbalize the story through a poster.

GRADE LEVEL: Primary — 3rd grade

TIME: Part I — 45 minutes; Part II — 30 minutes; Part III — 60 minutes

NUMBER: Best played with a maximum of 16 students

METHOD OF CHECKING: Teacher

MATERIALS:
1) Caldecott books — one for each student participating.
2) Many varied magazine, newspaper or catalog pictures.
3) Art supplies — colored paper, colored posterboard, crayons, paints, colored pencils, assorted felt-tip pens, charcoal, felt squares, scraps of material, and so on.
4) Paper and pencils — enough for each student.

PROCEDURE:
PART I
1) Pass out a Caldecott book to each player who should read the book thoroughly.
2) On a sheet of paper, write down: a) author and title, b) the main characters and a description of each, and c) a paragraph telling about the story.
3) Students are to choose suitable pictures to portray the characters and story lines of their books. If suitable pictures cannot be found, they may be drawn and colored or painted.
4) When all the pictures have been gathered together, use them to discuss the books.

PART II
1) Make available all types of art materials.
2) Discuss with the students the worth of posters and why they are important to advertise important aspects of an event, book, movie, and so on.
3) Using the pictures and/or drawn pictures, have each student make a poster that will "sell" his/her book to other members of the class. Make sure the author and title are mentioned.

PART III

1) Students, with their posters, are to arrange themselves in a circle on the floor.

2) Each student is to pick his/her favorite character from the book and tell the story as if he/she were that character. Students should keep in mind that they are trying to convince others to read their books.

3) Pick one student to begin and then continue around the circle.

4) Display finished work around the room.

5) Students are to walk around the room and decide which poster best depicts the book portrayed.

6) By Australian ballot, vote on the best poster and story. If they do not agree, vote separately.

7) Pin a first, second and third place ribbon on the winning posters. If the storytelling vote differs from the poster vote, issue a first, second and third place ribbon to the storytellers.

■ ■ ■

◄►◄►◄►◄►◄►◄►◄►◄►◄►◄►◄►◄►◄►◄►◄►◄►◄►◄►
TIC-TAC-TOE TITLES
◄►◄►◄►◄►◄►◄►◄►◄►◄►◄►◄►◄►◄►◄►◄►◄►◄►◄►

PURPOSE: To help students recall book characters and correctly identify the titles of books in which they are found. To motivate students to read books that might appeal to them.

GRADE LEVEL: 3rd grade through 5th grade

TIME: 30 minutes

NUMBER: Best played with a maximum of 16 students

METHOD OF CHECKING: Teacher

MATERIALS:
1) Chalkboard, chalk, and erasers.
2) Master list of "character clues."
3) Dittoed list of book titles.
4) Large manila envelope (10x13-inches) for the materials.

PROCEDURE:
1) In the period before this game is to be played, give each student a dittoed list of titles to study and urge them to become familiar with the characters.
2) Divide the students into two evenly matched teams. Each team is to pick a captain.
3) Draw a Tic-Tac-Toe board on the chalkboard.
4) The team whose captain's last name is closest to the beginning of the alphabet begins. If two initials are the same, go to the second letter.
5) The captain has a chance to choose the symbol for the team to use — the "X" or "O."
6) The teacher is to read a clue, from a master list, as to the identity of a book character.

7) The first team is to identify the character from the clue. If correct, the student who provides the answer goes to the board and fills in either an "X" or an "O" depending what symbol the captain has chosen.

8) If incorrect, play passes to the opposing team and the first player to raise his/her hand gives the book title. If neither team gives the correct answer, go on to another "clue" and come back to that one.

9) Teams continue taking turns until one team completes a row diagonally, vertically or horizontally.

10) Play starts over once a team has won a match.

11) The team that wins the most matches of Tic-Tac-Toe wins the tournament.

■ ■ ■

PURPOSE: To enable students to recognize authors and titles of recent works.

GRADE LEVEL: Intermediate — 4th grade

TIME: 25 minutes

NUMBER: Best played with a maximum of 16 students

METHOD OF CHECKING: Game leader/teacher

MATERIALS:

1   24 4x8-inch colored posterboard title cards.

2) 2 sets of 24 3x3-inch colored posterboard author cards, one for each team. The sets should be in different colors. A suggested list:

Author	Title
Arthur, R. M.	*On the Wasteland*
Babbitt, Natalie	*Tuck Everlasting*
Carroll, Lewis	*Hunting of the Snark*
Doty, Jean	*Summer Pony*
Eager, Edward	*Knight's Castle*
Fleischman, Sid	*McBroom's Ghost*
Gage, Wilson	*Secret of Crossbone Hill*
Hoban, Russell	*Sea Thing Child*
James, Will	*Smoky*
Kendall, Carol	*Whisper of Glocken*
Lindgrin, Astrid	*Pippi Longstocking*
Maxwell, R. H.	*Cowboy on Ice*
Norton, Mary	*Borrowers Afloat*
O'Dell, Scott	*Island of the Blue Dolphins*
Peck, Robert	*Soup and Me*
Rawls, Wilson	*Where the Red Fern Grows*
Sawyer, Ruth	*Enchanted Schoolhouse*
Snyder, Zilpha	*Until the Celebration*
Stolz, Mary	*Noonday Friends*
Taylor, Sydney	*All of a Kind Family*
Travers, Pamela	*Mary Poppins*
Wahl, Jan	*How the Children Stopped the Wars*
Warner, Gertrude	*Surprise Island*
Young, Miriam	*Witch Mobile*

3) Master list of authors and titles.

4) Dittoed list of titles and authors — one for each student.

5) Large manila envelope (12x15-inches) for the materials.

PROCEDURE:

1) The period before this game is to be played, give each student a dittoed list of titles and authors to study.

2) Divide the students into two evenly matched teams. Each team is to pick a captain.

3) One player is chosen as game leader and given a set of title cards.

4) One set of the matching author cards is passed to the captains of each team who then distributes the cards to team members. Each player should receive three cards.

5) The teams line up behind the captains on one side of the room.

6) The game leader is placed at the opposite side of the room.

7) The game leader holds up a title card.

8) One player from each team, who thinks she/he has the author card, must *walk* to the game leader and tag his/her hand.

9) Whichever player tags the hand first gets a point if the answer is correct.

10) If correct, the author card is left with the game leader and placed in a pile either to his/her left or right depending on placement of team. If incorrect, the player returns, with the card, to the team to try again.

11) The teacher is to be by the game leader, with the master list, in case a dispute over who is right arises.

12) The team who has deposited the most author cards with the game leader wins the match.

■ ■ ■

◄► ◄► ◄► ◄► ◄► ◄► ◄► ◄► ◄► ◄► ◄► ◄► ◄► ◄► ◄► ◄► ◄► ◄► ◄►

ZIP-ZAP

◄► ◄► ◄► ◄► ◄► ◄► ◄► ◄► ◄► ◄► ◄► ◄► ◄► ◄► ◄► ◄► ◄► ◄►

PURPOSE: To acquaint students with the titles of Newbery Medal winners.

GRADE LEVEL: Intermediate — 5th and 6th grades

TIME: 30 minutes

NUMBER: Best played with a maximum of 16 students

METHOD OF CHECKING: Self-checking

MATERIALS:
1) Book cart on which have been placed Newbery titles.

PROCEDURE:
1) Familiarize students with the Newbery titles assigning one title to each student.

2) Students sit in a circle around a player in the center.

3) Players memorize the Newbery titles to their right and left sides; Zip on left, Zap on right.

4) Player in the middle calls out "Zip-Zap," points to a person, and starts counting to 10 fast.

5) The player pointed to must answer with the titles before the count of 10 or become the person in the center.

6) Play continues in this fashion until every player has had a turn or time is called.

■ ■ ■

TITLE TUTOR RELAY

PURPOSE: To acquaint students with certain authors and book titles.

GRADE LEVEL: Intermediate—4th and 5th grades

TIME: 25 minutes

NUMBER: Best played with a maximum of 16 students

METHOD OF CHECKING: Teacher

MATERIALS:
1) 16 sets of 3 2x6-inch colored posterboard cards. Each card bears the name of an author and the title of his/her book, and is cut so as to form jigsaw pieces.

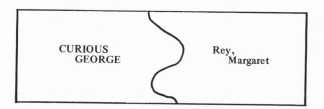

Titles	Authors
Sea Full of Whales	Richard Armour
What Makes the Sun Shine	Isaac Asimov
Deenie	Judy Blume
Paddington Abroad	Michael Bond
Katie John	Mary Calhoun
Grover	Vera Cleaver
Magic Finger	Roald Dahl
The Masked Monkey	Frank Dixon
Pandas Live Here	Irmengarde Eberle
Prehistoric Animals	Sam Epstein
Story of Persephone	Penelope Farmer
The Warlock of Westfall	Leonard Fisher
Exploring Mars	Roy Gallant
Art of the Southwest Indians	Shirley Glubok
Doctor J	James Haskins
All about Horses	Marguerite Henry
Riddle of Stegosaurus	D. C. Ipsen
Naturecraft	Carol Inouye
Antique Cars	Robert Jackson
Phantom Tollbooth	Norton Juster

(List continues on page 232)

Titles (cont'd)	**Authors (cont'd)**
Secret of Mirror Bay	Carolyn Keene
Big Red	James Kjelgaard
Story of World War II	Robert Leckie
Orange Is a Color	Sharon Lerner
One Frog Too Many	Mercer Mayer
Come on Seabiscuit	Ralph Moody
The Complete Book of Dragons	E. Nesbit
Exiles of the Stars	Alice Norton
The Church Mouse	Graham Oakley
Mystery in the Old Red Barn	Helen Orton
Haunted House	Peggy Parish
The Tale of Squirrel Nutkin	Beatrix Potter
Figgs and Phantoms	Ellen Raskin
How to Eat Fried Worms	Thomas Rockwell
Truth about Mary Rose	Marilyn Sachs
Black Beauty	Anna Sewell
Air Raid: Pearl Harbor	Theodore Taylor
Anatole and the Toyshop	Eve Titus
Tiger up a Tree	Kurt Unkelbach
Sunflower Garden	Janice Udry
Mysterious Island	Jules Verne
Little Brown Bat	Virginia Voight
How the Children Stopped the Wars	Jan Wahl
Clay, Wood and Wire	Harvey Weiss
The Girl Who Cried Flowers	Jane Yolen
Zoo Was My World	Wesley Young
Sharks	Herbert Zim
Sugar Mouse Cake	Gene Zion

2) 16 6x9-inch envelopes for the puzzle pieces, numbered on the outside to correspond to the numbers on the back of the puzzle pieces.

3) Large manila envelope (16x20-inches) for the materials.

PURPOSE:

1) Divide the students into two evenly matched teams.

2) A team captain is appointed who becomes the first player on a team. Other team members line up behind him.

3) The first two players on the team are each given an envelope with three Title Tutor Relay cards in them.

4) Players must match the halves of all three cards, then shuffle and replace them in the envelope, and pass them to the person behind.

5) While the second player is matching the cards, the first player receives another set of cards.

6) This procedure continues with the first players receiving as many envelopes as there are players on the team. If there are eight team members, each player matches 24 cards.

7) The team that finishes first is the winner.

8) The teacher, throughout the entire game, is circulating to see that everything is proceeding correctly.

◄►

MAGNEATO

◄►

PURPOSE: To allow students to check their own comprehension of books.

GRADE LEVEL: Intermediate—4th grade through 6th grade

TIME: 25 minutes

NUMBER: Best played with a maximum of 16 students

METHOD OF CHECKING: Answer sheet

MATERIALS:
  1) 4 Magneato gameboards made of 20x14-inch colored posterboard.

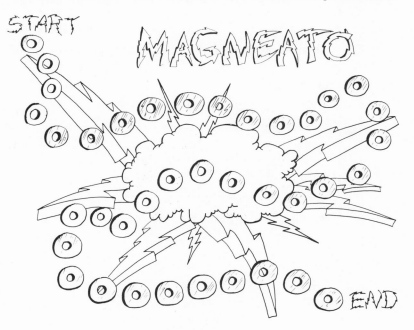

  2) 4 sets of 35 3x4-inch colored posterboard cards bearing questions. Each set should be for a different book. A total of 140 cards will be needed. Each set should be numbered on the reverse side. Sample questions:

  Why did Henry Huggins sell earthworms?
  What did Henry call his dog?
  How did Henry finally get the dog on the bus?

(Materials list continues on page 234)

3) 3 Magneato cards to a set, for a total of 12 cards:

   Go back 3 spaces
   Go ahead 2 spaces
   Go to start

4) Master list of questions and answers dry-mounted to a piece of colored posterboard.

5) 16 magnets to be used as markers. Magnets with flowers or fruit make colorful markers.

6) 4 spinners.

7) Large manila envelope (16x20-inches) for the materials.

PROCEDURE:

1) Groups of four are formed by counting off in fours.

2) Each group is given a Magneato gameboard and related materials.

3) Players place markers on the gameboard and spin to determine the order of play.

4) The first player spins, draws a card, and answers the question.

5) The other players may check the answer sheet for the correct answer.

6) If correct, the player moves the number of spaces indicated on the spinner. If incorrect, the player does not move, and the next player takes a turn.

7) Play continues in this manner with players alternating turns.

8) The first player to reach the end wins.

■ ■ ■

WHO SAID IT???

PURPOSE: To help students gain self-confidence in using their knowledge of literature.

GRADE LEVEL: Intermediate—4th grade through 6th grade

TIME: 25 minutes

NUMBER: Best played with a maximum of 16 students

METHOD OF CHECKING: Teacher

MATERIALS:
1) 32 3x4-inch colored posterboard cards bearing quotations.

2) Master list of quotations and characters dry-mounted to a piece of colored posterboard. Some examples are:

"None of your beeswax."—Henry Huggins

"Mirror, Mirror on the wall,
Who is the fairest of them all?"—Witch from *Snow White*

"In the Spring when we get back,
I'll go to school as Miss Glinka,
a new substitute teacher."—Glenda

"I wish I had a brain."—Scarecrow from *Wizard of Oz*

"No, we have to go on Wednesday.
I'll write you full details of my plan.
You must show the plan to no one.
Memorize all the details; then destroy my note."—Claudia *From the Mixed Up Files of Mrs. Basil E. Frankweiler*

"Send me back to Kansas."—Dorothy from *Wizard of Oz*

"Now," she said, "spit-spot into bed."—Mary Poppins

"So long boys," she said, "don't you worry about me.
I'll always come out on top."—Pippi Longstocking

3) Large manila envelope (10x13-inches) for the materials.

PROCEDURE:
1) Players form two teams by counting off in twos, choose captains, and sit behind the captains facing the teacher.

2) The teacher designates the starting team and shuffles the cards.

(Procedures continue on page 236)

3) The first player draws a card from the pile held by the teacher and has one minute to identify the character from the quotation given.

4) If correct, the team scores a point. If incorrect, or if no answer is given, team 2 has an opportunity to score an extra point by answering correctly.

5) If neither team answers correctly, the teacher gives the answer and neither team scores a point.

6) Play continues in this manner with teams alternating turns.

7) The team with the most points wins.

■ ■ ■

◀▶ ◀▶ ◀▶ ◀▶ ◀▶ ◀▶ ◀▶ ◀▶ ◀▶ ◀▶ ◀▶ ◀▶ ◀▶ ◀▶ ◀▶ ◀▶ ◀▶

ROSTER RELAY

◀▶ ◀▶ ◀▶ ◀▶ ◀▶ ◀▶ ◀▶ ◀▶ ◀▶ ◀▶ ◀▶ ◀▶ ◀▶ ◀▶ ◀▶ ◀▶ ◀▶

PURPOSE: To help students recall information pertaining to books and authors.

GRADE LEVEL: Intermediate—4th grade through 6th grade

TIME: 30 minutes

NUMBER: Best played with a maximum of 16 students

METHOD OF CHECKING: Teacher

MATERIALS:
1) Chalkboard, chalk, and eraser.
2) Master list of categories dry-mounted to a piece of colored poster-board. Sample categories:

   Titles with animal names
   Titles of science fiction
   Authors of picture books
   Names of animal characters
   Boys who are main characters
   Girls who are main characters

3) Timer.
4) Large manila envelope (10x13-inches) for the materials.

PROCEDURE:
1) Form two teams by counting off in twos and choose two captains.
2) The teams line up behind the captains facing the chalkboard.
3) The teacher writes the category on the board and sets the timer for 10 minutes. (Example: Names of animal characters).
4) The first player on each team walks to the chalkboard, writes the name of an animal character, gives the chalk to the next player and goes to the end of the line.
5) If a player cannot think of a name of an animal character, an "X" is placed on the chalkboard.
6) Players continue in this manner until the timer rings.
7) Two points are scored for each correct name listed. One point is subtracted for each "X."
8) Play resumes with a new category. Points are cumulative and the team with the most points wins.

237

NAME THAT CHARACTER

PURPOSE: To acquaint students with books and the characters found within them.

GRADE LEVEL: Intermediate — 4th grade through 6th grade

TIME: 30 minutes

NUMBER: Best played with a maximum of 16 students

METHOD OF CHECKING: Teacher

MATERIALS:
1) 2 bells and 1 timer.
2) Master list of titles, characters, and questions dry-mounted to a piece of colored posterboard. Some sample questions are:
   Charlotte's Web — Charlotte — Who had the ability to write and thus saved a pig from death?

   Mr. Popper's Penguins — Mr. Popper — Who was the house painter who longed to go exploring and kept penguins in the ice box?

   Madeline — Madeline — What little girl lived in a school with eleven other little girls?

   Little Toot — Little Toot — What small boat rescued a big ocean liner?
3) Dittoed lists of titles and characters — one for each student.
4) 2 tables.
5) Pencils and paper for scorekeeping.
6) Large manila envelope (12x15-inches) for the materials.

PROCEDURE:
1) In the period before this game is to be played, give each student a dittoed list of titles and characters to study.
2) Divide the students into two evenly matched teams. Each team is to choose a captain.
3) The bells are placed on the tables.
4) Teams line up on one side of the tables with the captains on the opposite side, keeping score.

5) The teacher stands between the tables with the master list for questioning.

6) The first player on each team steps up to the table, places hands at his/her side and waits for the clue.

7) The timer is set for 1 minute and the clue is given.

8) The first player to ring the bell, within the time allowance, is given a chance to identify the character who fits the description and to give the title of the book.

9) If correct, the team scores one point, and both players go to the end of the lines. If incorrect, the opposing player is given a chance to answer. If neither player is correct, the teacher can either give the correct answer or use the description another time.

10) The next two players step up and the same procedure is repeated.

11) The team with the most points wins.

■ ■ ■

PURPOSE: To familiarize students with a list of titles and authors.

GRADE LEVEL: Intermediate — 5th and 6th grades

TIME: Part I — 30 minutes; Part II — 25 minutes; Part III — 45 minutes; Part IV — 50 minutes

NUMBER: Best played with a maximum of 16 students

METHOD OF CHECKING: Teacher

MATERIALS:
1) Paper for recording authors and titles.
2) 32 colored strips for shelf markers made of posterboard or any other durable material.
3) 1 timer.
4) List of 10-15 activities for presentation of books. The following are possible activities.

> *Booklets* — One student may make a booklet, or several students who have read the same book may make pages and put them all together. a) Have the students draw a picture presenting an event or character in the book and write a short caption beneath it telling why it was an important part of the story. b) The booklet may be made by writing something on the left hand page and illustrating the idea on the right hand page.

> *Dioramas* —

> *Shoe box projects* — The background is made on the sides of the box. There are stand-up figures on the box lid.

> *Simple diorama* — a) Have the students make the picture, b) make the frame, c) make the people and things for the foreground, and d) put it all together. The picture is the background and the people are pasted to the frame to stand up in the front.

> *Box diorama* — The box is open at the front and the top. The back and sides are the background, the figures come in the foreground.

> *Mosaics* — Have the students tear small pieces of colored paper and paste them on a background paper leaving space between each piece for the background to show through. This may depict a main event or several main characters from the book. Write a short paragraph telling about the mosaics.

Riddle Box—Fill a box with riddles about stories. Describe a book and then ask what the title is. Or give the title in the riddle and describe a character from that book, asking the name of the character. Example: "I am a book about a girl who has many adventures with a scarecrow, a tin man, and a lion. What book am I? (*Wizard of Oz*). Example: "I am in the *Wizard of Oz*. I thought I had no heart. What character am I?" (The Tin Woodsman).

5) Art materials for students to work with.

6) 16 sets of 3 2x6-inch colored posterboard cards, bearing authors and titles and cut to form jigsaw pieces.

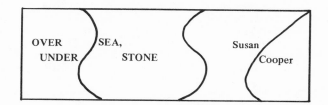

Titles	Authors
Over Sea, Under Stone	Susan Cooper
Island of the Blue Dolphin	Scott O'Dell
M. C. Higgins the Great	Virginia Hamilton
Eye in the Forest	Mary Steele
The Gray King	Susan Cooper
Mrs. Frisby and the Rats of Nimh	Robert O'Brien
Sounder	William Armstrong
From the Mixed Up Files of Mrs. Basil E. Frankweiler	Elaine Konigsburg
A Wrinkle in Time	Madeleine L'Engle
The Bronze Bow	Elizabeth Speare
A Wind in the Door	Madeleine L'Engle
Witch of Blackbird Pond	Elizabeth Speare
Wheel on the School	Meindert De Jong
Secret of the Andes	Ann Clark
Red Hart Magic	Andre Norton
Walk out of the World	Ruth Nichols
Runaway Stallion	Walter Morey
Caddie Woodlawn	Carol Brink
Flight to Lonesome Place	Alexander Key
The Whispering Knights	Penelope Lively
Deenie	Judy Blume
Beat the Turtle Drum	Constance Greene
The Door in the Wall	Marguerite De Angeli
Call It Courage	Armstrong Sperry

(List continues on page 242)

Titles (cont'd)	Authors (cont'd)
The Twenty-One Balloons	William Du Bois
Strawberry Girl	Lois Lenski
Rabbit Hill	Robert Lawson
The Matchlock Gun	Walter Edmonds
The White Stag	Kate Seredy
Magic or Not	Eager Edwards
Black Penny	Phoebe Erickson
The Black Stallion	Walter Farley
Lion, the Witch and the Wardrobe	C. S. Lewis
Below the Root	Zilpha Snyder
Cat in the Mirror	Mary Stolz
Little House on the Prairie	Laura I. Wilder
Dobry	Monica Shannon
Invincible Louisa	Cornelia Meigs
Voyages of Doctor Dolittle	Hugh Lofting
Centerburg Tales	Robert McCloskey
The Shattered Stone	Robert Newman
Little Women	Louisa May Alcott
A Bear Called Paddington	Michael Bond
Stones of Green Knowe	Lucy Boston
Wind in the Willows	Kenneth Grahame
Navajo Slave	Lynne Gessner
Smoky	Will James
Astercote	Penelope Lively
Heidi	Johanna Spyri
The Hobbit	J. R. R. Tolkien

7) 16 6x9-inch manila envelopes to keep the puzzle pieces in, numbered on the outside to correspond to the numbers on the backs of the puzzle pieces.

8) Small box for the materials.

PROCEDURE:

PART I

1) Divide the students into two evenly matched teams. Once in teams, the students are to form pairs.

2) Each pair of players receives an envelope of author-title puzzle cards.

3) The paired players put the puzzles together and write down the titles and authors.

4) When step 3 is completed, the puzzle pieces are shuffled and placed back in the envelope. The envelope is then traded with a pair of players from the opposing team.

5) This procedure continues until all puzzles have been completed or time runs out, and all titles and authors have been recorded.

6) The team that finishes first or has the most authors and titles recorded wins.

PART II

1) Before this part is played, the teacher should make a master list of the recorded author-titles, for both teams. From this list the teacher can easily check the books placed on the team tables to make sure they are the ones recorded.

2) The team is to choose a pair of players to remain at the "team table" and alphabetize the books when they are placed on the table.

3) Each pair of players takes a sheet of author-titles that they have recorded in Part I, and goes to the shelves to find the books bearing the authors' names. Players agree to hunt for the author-titles of the pair remaining at the "team table."

4) A timer is set for 15 minutes.

5) When the book is found, it is placed on the "team table" where one team member will begin to alphabetize the books according to the authors' last names.

6) When the timer goes off, all team members gather around their "team table" to wait until their books have been checked by the teacher.

7) For each book found, the team scores 1 point. If the books, at the end of the search, are in correct alphabetical order, add an extra 5 points to the total.

8) Once the books have been checked, the players are to choose one of them to read by the next meeting (usually 1-2 weeks elapse between meetings).

9) The books not chosen by the players are to be reshelved, in alphabetical order, and colored strips inserted beside them so the teacher may check to see if they are placed correctly.

PART III

1) From a prepared list of activities, the players are to choose a method by which to present their books to the section.

2) Once the activity is chosen, the rest of the period may be spent working on the project.

3) If it is not finished in the time allowed, the project is taken home and finished by the next meeting.

PART IV

Oral presentation of projects.

■ ■ ■

TIC-TAC-TOE WITH AUTHORS

PURPOSE: To familiarize students with authors and with different types of books.

GRADE LEVEL: Intermediate—6th grade

TIME: 10-15 minutes per round

NUMBER: Best played with a maximum of 16 students

METHOD OF CHECKING: Teacher

MATERIALS:
1) Chalkboard, chalk, and eraser. An example of categories for the Tic-Tac-Toe board:

SCIENCE FICTION	HORSE STORIES	SPORTS
ADOLESCENT PROBLEMS	FANTASY	MYSTERY
POTPOURRI	ADVENTURE	SPACE AND TIME

2) Master list of authors, categories, and clues dry-mounted to a piece of colored posterboard.

3) A coin of any denomination.

4) Large manila envelope (10x13-inches) for the materials.

PROCEDURE:
1) Divide the students into two evenly matched teams; choose team captains.

2) The captain becomes team spokesman and makes all the decisions for the team.

3) The team captain whose last name is closest to the beginning of the alphabet is first to call "heads" or "tails" and flips the coin. Whichever leader calls the flip correctly begins.

4) The captain consults the team and selects a category from the Tic-Tac-Toe board.

5) The teacher or an appointed student asks team 1 a question about the category selected.

6) The captain may answer or choose a teammate to answer the question (preferably one who has volunteered).

7) Once the captain has selected the person to answer, no one else may assist in answering.

8) The first answer is accepted. If the answer is correct, an "X" or "O" is placed in the square. If the student answers incorrectly, team 2 has the opportunity to answer the question.

9) If team 2 accepts the challenge and answers the question correctly, they get that square and then select another category for a possible two in a row. If, however, they answer incorrectly they do not receive a second category and the turn goes back to team 1.

10) No team may earn an "X" or "O" without answering a question correctly.

11) If team 2 decides, however, not to answer the other team's missed question, they select their own category, but do not get a second turn.

12) The first team to score three "X"s or three "O"s in a row, horizontally, vertically, or diagonally, wins the game.

13) In the event no team completes a row, the team with the most "X"s and "O"s wins the game.

PURPOSE: To help students identify Newbery authors.

GRADE LEVEL: Intermediate—4th and 5th grades

TIME: Part I—90 minutes; Part II—30 minutes

NUMBER: Best played with a maximum of 16 students

METHOD OF CHECKING: Teacher

MATERIALS:

1) 32 4x8-inch colored posterboard labels with authors' names printed on them in black felt-tip pen; 16 cards per set, for a total of 2 sets.

Set I	Set II
Ellen Raskin	Katherine Paterson
Susan Cooper	Mildred Taylor
Virginia Hamilton	Paula Fox
Jean Craighead George	Robert O'Brien
William Armstrong	E. L. Konigsburg
Lloyd Alexander	Irene Hunt
Madeleine L'Engle	Robert Lawson
Ann Nolan Clark	Meindert De Jong
Harold Keith	Elizabeth Speare
Joseph Krumgold	Scott O'Dell
Marguerite De Angeli	Elizabeth Yates
William Du Bois	Marguerite Henry
Lois Lenski	Esther Forbes
Elizabeth Gray	Walter Edmonds
Armstrong Sperry	Cornelia Meigs
Kate Seredy	James Daugherty

2) 32 pieces of strong or yarn, 12 inches to 14 inches long, to put through the tops of the author labels so they will slip over students' heads and hang on their backs.

3) Book cart with the following reference works or others that include the same types of information:

   Junior Book of Authors
   More Junior Authors
   Third Book of Junior Authors
   Something About the Authors
   Yesterday's Authors of Books for Children

4) One dittoed sheet listing the authors' names for each student.

5) Master list of authors, Newbery titles, and facts about the authors. For example:

Susan Cooper— *The Grey King* —She was educated at Somerville College, Oxford, where she was the first woman ever to edit the university newspaper. Her books are mainly fiction and she feels closest of all to the theme of the ancient magic of England.

6) 1 timer.

7) Large manila envelope (12x15-inches) for the materials.

PROCEDURE:

PART I

1) Each student is given a copy of the list of authors and must write a concise description of the author's life and works by looking through appropriate reference books.

2) Students may work in pairs or in groups of three and exchange the descriptions in preparation for an oral presentation.

3) After each presentation, the class and the teacher should ask questions to clarify the author description.

4) Students are to study their sheets in preparation for Part II.

PART II

1) Divide the students into two evenly matched teams and choose a leader for each.

2) Team leaders are to ask the teacher for author labels for the team members. Labels are to be placed over the team members' heads to hang on their backs. The teacher places the label on the team leader.

3) When all labels are in place, the timer is set for 25 minutes.

4) Members of team 1 must ask questions of members of team 2 to learn their own identities. Team 2 follows the same procedure as team 1.

5) When a team member learns her/his identity, she/he tells the teacher who gives her/him a new label and scores a point for the team.

6) Stress honesty among team members not to give away identities.

7) The team with the most points at the end of 25 minutes are declared the best searchers and fact finders.

■ ■ ■

— APPENDIX —

DESCRIPTIONS OF REFERENCE BOOKS
USED IN THE GAMES

Bartlett, John, ed. *Bartlett's Familiar Quotations*. Boston: Little, Brown, 1968.

Gives the source of each quotation listed.

Brewton, John E., and Sara Brewton, comps. *Index to Children's Poetry*. New York: H. W. Wilson, 1942. *First Supplement*, 1954; *Second Supplement*, 1965.

Original volume is a dictionary index of 130 collections of poems for children and youth — with title, author, subject and first line entries. Supplements index 66 and 85 collections respectively. Their 1972 volume, entitled *Index to Poetry for Children and Young People: 1964-1969* treats 117 more collections.

Children's Literature Review, Vol. I, II, and III. Detroit, MI: Gale Research Co., 1976— (irreg.).

Arranged in alphabetical order by the author's last name, giving an excerpt of recent reviews of both fiction and non-fiction for children and young people.

Commire, Anne, ed. *Something About the Author*. Detroit, MI: Gale Research Co., 1971— .

Facts and pictures about contemporary authors and illustrators of books for young people.

Commire, Anne, ed. *Yesterday's Authors of Books for Children* (2 vols.). Detroit, MI: Gale Research Co., 1977. Vol. 3, 1979.

Facts and pictures about authors and illustrators of books for young people from early times to 1960.

Couzens, Reginald. *The Stories of the Months and Days.* Detroit, MI: Gale Research Co., 1971.

Provides the myths and legends behind the names of the months and days of the week. The attributes, feats, and significance of the gods and heroes whose names adorn the calendar are explained also.

Evans, Ivor, ed. *Brewer's Dictionary of Phrase and Fable.* New York: Harper and Row, 1971.

An extensive alphabetical list of classical references. Contains some slang phrases and expressions that arose from World War II.

Fuller, Muriel. *More Junior Authors.* New York: H. W. Wilson, 1963.

Supplements *The Junior Book of Authors* with 268 biographical and autobiographical sketches and 249 portraits.

Funk, Wilfred. *Word Origins and Their Romantic Stories.* New York: Funk and Wagnalls, 1950.

Shows the life history of a word, which makes its present meaning clearer. Arranged in chapters dealing with certain areas of life such as house, garden, politics, and so on.

Grant, Bruce. *The Cowboy Encyclopedia.* New York: Rand McNally, 1968 (pa.).

An extensive alphabetical listing which brings together the most important and interesting facts about cowboys. Describes the old and new West from the open range to the dude ranch.

Halliburton, Richard. *Book of Marvels.* New York: Bobbs-Merrill, 1941.

This book is filled with pictures of the world's cities, mountains, temples, and maps to show where they are located. The information is related in storybook style.

Hone, William. *The Every-Day Book* (2 vols.). Detroit, MI: Gale Research Co., 1967.

For every day of the year there are articles, poems, historical notes, essays on folklore and customs, religious information, and illustrations.

Illustrated Encyclopedia of the Animal Kingdom. Danbury, CT: Grolier Inc., 1972. (20 vols.).

This encyclopedia covers in detail, all the major groups of animals, their appearance and ancestry, their geographic distribution, their living habits and relationships to the world at large.

Jordan, E. L. *Animal Atlas of the World.* Maplewood, NJ: Hammond Inc., 1969.

This work combines animal portraits, descriptive text and range maps, together with its survey of the most famous nature preserves on five continents, attributes of wildlife and geography.

Kane, Joseph. *Famous First Facts.* New York: H. W. Wilson Co., 1964.

An alphabetical listing of the first time that something happened.

Kingman, Lee, ed. *Newbery & Caldecott Medal Books: 1966-1975.* Boston: Horn Book Inc., 1975.

For each year there is an excerpt from the book, a short summary of the work, and the acceptance speech by the author.

Kravitz, David. *Who's Who in Greek and Roman Mythology.* New York: Clarkson Potter, 1977.

An alphabetical listing of mythological characters with entries that emphasize and clarify intrafamily relationships.

Kunitz, Stanley, and Howard Haycraft, eds. *Junior Book of Authors.* New York: H. W. Wilson Co., 1951.

Biographical and autobiographical sketches of authors and illustrators of books for children and young people.

McWhirter, Norris. *Guinness Book of World Records.* New York: Bantam Books, 1978.

Claims to include the greatest human achievements of the century. The book uses a table of contents and an index to arrange the material.

Melbo, Irving. *Our Country's National Parks* (2 vols.). New York: Bobbs-Merrill, 1973.

A story of all national parks presenting historical, factual, and scientific information.

Montreville, Doris de, and Donna Hill, eds. *Third Book of Junior Authors.* New York: H. W. Wilson Co., 1972.

Sketches of authors are in alphabetical order by the form of author's name appearing most frequently on title pages.

Morris, Richard B., and Jeffrey B. Morris, eds. *Encyclopedia of American History.* New York: Harper and Row, 1976.

One volume of essential historical facts in both chronological and topical order. Dates, events, achievements, and persons of importance are given in narrative form.

National Geographic Index, 1947-1976. Washington, DC: National Geographic Society, 1977.

An alphabetical listing of more than 14,000 entries spanning 30 years, this helps find information on different articles.

National Geographic Picture Atlas of Our Fifty States. Ed. by Margaret Sedeen. Washington, DC: National Geographic Society, 1978.

With the map of each state there is a state story and a quick summary of economic facts. In addition, there are many drawings, photographs and graphs placed in strategic positions.

New Book of Popular Science. Danbury, CT: Grolier Inc., 1978. (6 vols.).

Discusses the major sciences and their application to today's world.

Ocean World of Jacques Cousteau. Danbury, CT: Grolier Inc., 1975. (20 vols.).

An exploration of the ocean's existence, how it moves and breathes, how it is effected by the seasons, how it nourishes its hosts of living things, how it harmonizes the physical and biological rhythms of the whole earth.

Palmer, Robin. *A Dictionary of Mythical Places.* New York: Walch, 1975.

An alphabetically arranged dictionary of mythical, legendary, and famous places briefly describing the origin, location, and major characteristics of each place.

Roget, Peter M. *Roget's Thesaurus of English Words and Phrases.* Ed. by R. A. Dutch. New York: St. Martin's Press, 1965.

An alphabetical listing of words with synonyms.

Ross, Frank. *Stories of the States.* New York: Crowell, 1969.

An alphabetical listing of the fifty states and the United States' territories, giving major characteristics of each and a short history.

Schiller, Andrew, and William A. Jenkins. *Junior Thesaurus: In Other Words II.* Rev. ed. New York: Lothrop, Lee and Shepard, 1978.

An alphabetical listing of words with synonyms and their meanings.

Shaw, John M. *Childhood in Poetry* (5 vols.). Detroit, MI: Gale Research Co., 1967. *First Supplement* (3 vols.), 1972; *Second Suppplement* (2 vols.), 1976.

A catalog with biographical and critical annotations of the books of English and American poets comprising the Shaw Childhood in Poetry Collection in the library of Florida State University.

Webster's Biographical Dictionary. Springfield, MA: G. & C. Merriam Co., 1976.

An alphabetical listing of famous people, past and present. This single volume work provides biographical references not restricted in its selection of names by considerations of historical period, nationality, race, religion or occupation, and it supplies the reader with full information on the syllabic division and the pronunciation of the names included.

Webster's New Geographical Dictionary. Rev. ed. Springfield, MA: G. & C. Merriam Co., 1977.

Entries were selected on the basis of usefulness and interest to the general reader, and include the world's independent states, dependencies, major administrative subdivisions, largest cities and significant natural physical features listed in alphabetical order.

Worrelle, Estelle. *Early American Costume.* Harrisburg, PA: Stackpole Books, 1975.

Each chapter gives a description of the period's costumes and a picture, starting in 1580 and ending in 1850.

Worth, Fred L. *The Trivia Encyclopedia.* Los Angeles: Brooke House, 1974.

An alphabetical listing of interesting and trivial facts that are difficult to find elsewhere.

ABOUT THE AUTHORS

Irene W. Bell, 1944- . Born in New York City, she holds degrees from the State University College at Potsdam, New York (B.A. in Social Sciences), the University of Massachusetts (M.A. in American History), and the University of Denver (M.A. in Librarianship). A former junior high school history teacher with the Ipswich, MA Public Schools, she is now a Media Specialist (K-6) with the Denver Public Schools. Ms. Bell has currently completed a series of workshops for the State Department of Education (Wyoming) on "Gaming: An Alternative to Teaching Library Skills" and will be involved with the Association for Educational Communications & Technology (AECT) presenting "Gaming through Media." She is the co-author of *Basic Media Skills through Games* (Libraries Unlimited, 1979), and is engaged in writing a skills book for the junior high level. She is a member of the American Library Association (ALA) and the Colorado Educational Media Association (CEMA). At present, Ms. Bell resides in Littleton, Colorado, with her husband and three cats.

Jeanne E. Wieckert, 1939- . Born in Chicago, she holds degrees from the University of Northern Illinois (Education) and the University of Northern Colorado (Curriculum and Instruction with emphasis in International Education). A former Chicago Public School teacher, she is now a Media Specialist with the Denver Public Schools. Mrs. Wieckert has presented several workshops in the Colorado region as a result of her interest in affective education. She has recently received a grant to do further study in the area of teaching through gaming and is also involved in programming games from *Basic Media Skills through Games* (Libraries Unlimited, 1979) for computer use and in writing a skills book for the junior high level. She is a member of the American Library Association (ALA) and the Colorado Educational Media Association (CEMA). Mrs. Wieckert lives in Boulder County, Colorado, with her husband and two children.

INDEX OF GAME TITLES